Timeless Truths for Troubled Times

Wendi Gordon

DEDICATION

This book is dedicated to the glory of God and to my husband Steve, both of whom love me unconditionally and give me the strength to go on when I face troubled times.

ACKNOWLEDGMENTS

While the meditations in this book are written solely by me, we are all influenced by the people around us. With that in mind, I would like to express my gratitude to the people of St. Matthew Lutheran Church, Williamsport, Pennsylvania, the church I served as pastor before moving to Maui, and the people of Kihei Lutheran Church, Maui, Hawaii, my current church family, and its pastor, Dave Krueger. You have all helped me grow in faith, hope, and love, and given me rich experiences to draw from as I wrote these meditations. I thank God for you.

INTRODUCTION

To say that we live in troubled times is an understatement. There are massive street protests in countries around the world, the actions of terrorists have taken many lives and created an atmosphere of suspicion and fear, most government leaders seem more interested in protecting their own wealth and power (and that of the corporations who fund their campaigns) than in working together for the common good, and millions of people struggle to survive after losing their jobs or their retirement savings, their homes, their access to medical care, and their ability to feed their families.

Even if your own life has been relatively untouched by these realities, you probably have family members, friends, or co-workers who are not so fortunate. Newspapers, magazines, television, and the internet also bombard us with stories about how bad things are, and how difficult it will be to agree on solutions to the problems, much less implement them. How can we hold on to hope in these troubled times?

That question is both universal and deeply personal for me. My husband has been out of work for almost a year now, and I was laid off a couple of months ago. We are surviving for now, thanks to unemployment benefits and help from family and friends, but there are many questions about what the future holds for us and I worry about our financial situation. We used to joke that we would be able to retire two years after we die; that joke isn't so funny anymore.

My own efforts to find something to hold on to when everything seems to be falling apart, and to find words of hope in the midst of my despair, led me to the words of Scripture and other ancient texts. In the Psalms, especially, I found great comfort, because the full range of human emotions are expressed there. From angry tirades asking why God seems to be doing nothing and

1

demanding that God intervene to save lives and punish evildoers, to heartfelt cries of grief from those who feel hopeless and helpless, to shouts of joy and gratitude when times are good, the Psalms has it all. Jesus himself used words from the Psalms when he cried, "My God, my God, why have you forsaken me?"

What I realized as I read these texts is that while ancient writers certainly could not envision the details of the specific challenges facing the world today, the reality is that throughout history, humans have had to deal with corrupt leaders, wars, and fears about having enough food and other basic necessities to survive. Different cultures have always struggled to understand and accept each other, and there have always been those who put their own self-interests above what is best for everyone else.

There have also always been prophetic voices challenging us to love God and love our neighbors as ourselves, to resist the temptation to scapegoat others when times are tough, to work together to improve things, and to settle our differences without resorting to verbal or physical violence. My hope and prayer is that the ancient words of wisdom I have gathered in this book, and my reflections on how they relate to the difficulties we face now, will strengthen and encourage all who read these words, and inspire all of us to hold on to faith, hope, and love, and work together to make our world a better place.

Wendi Gordon
October 12, 2011

P.S. I have not grouped the meditations in any particular order; they do not necessarily need to be read consecutively. My suggestion is to read only one each day, and then take the time to reflect on what you have read and how it relates to your own life experience. I've concluded each meditation with questions for personal reflection; you may find it helpful to write your responses in a journal.

"For surely I know the plans I have for you, says the Lord, plans for your welfare and not for harm, to give you a future with hope."

Jeremiah 29:11

If I had to pick a single Bible verse as my favorite, it would probably be this one. I have it on a keychain, on my nightstand, and on a shelf in our living room. I refer to it often, especially when I'm not feeling very hopeful about the future.

It's important to understand this verse in context, though. The preceding verse reads, "For thus says the Lord: only when Babylon's seventy years are completed will I visit you, and I will fulfill to you my promise and bring you back to this place." God is speaking to the people sent into exile from Jerusalem to Babylon, telling them that one day they will return and their fortunes will be restored, *but only after seventy years of exile!*

Somehow I don't think that's the good news the people were hoping to hear. In fact, another prophet, Hananiah, was telling them that God would defeat the king of Babylon and rescue them within two years, and Jeremiah criticizes Hananiah for making the people trust in a lie.

One of the challenges facing us today is that we have leaders who tell us what we want to hear. Instead of helping us face some harsh realities and proposing realistic, long-term solutions, they promise quick fixes and reassure us that everything will be fine. The brave few who acknowledge the complexity of the problems we are facing and dare to suggest that major changes need to be made and that it won't be easy or inexpensive to make them usually don't remain in leadership positions for long.

I like this verse not only because it reassures me that God cares about my welfare and plans to give me a future with hope, but also because it reminds me that instant gratification isn't always possible or even desirable. When I am going through tough times, I get impatient and want God to magically make it all better right now, or at least tell me how and when my situation will improve. When I look back on other difficult periods in my life, though, I see that those times are often necessary for me to learn an important lesson, grow in my faith, or achieve something deeply meaningful to me. They also help me empathize with other people, and be caring and compassionate when I am in a position to help. In some cases, like when I didn't get a job I desperately wanted but then later got a different job for which I was much better suited, I can even see that what was a devastating experience at the time was actually a great blessing.

In my digital book *The Butterfly Principles: Nine Steps to Transform Your Life*, I tell the story of a man who watched a butterfly struggling to squeeze its body through a tiny opening in its cocoon. The man decided to help by carefully creating a larger opening, through which the butterfly soon emerged quite easily. However, it's wings were small and shriveled. What the man did not realize is that the process of squeezing its body through the tiny opening is what enables a butterfly to force fluid from its body into its wings and become capable of flight. Perhaps the same is true for humans: any transformation requires a period of struggle first.

Questions for Personal Reflection

1. Think about a difficult period in your past. What good came out of it? How were you changed by that experience, and how has it changed the way you respond to others facing similar situations?

2. Do you believe that God has plans for you? If so, what is God asking you to do to help those plans become a reality?

"Who will separate us from the love of Christ? Will hardship, or distress, or persecution, or famine, or nakedness, or peril, or sword? No, in all these things we are more than conquerors through him who loved us. For I am convinced that neither death, nor life, nor angels, nor rulers, nor things present, nor things to come, nor powers, nor height, nor depth, nor anything else in all creation, will be able to separate us from the love of God in Christ Jesus our Lord."

Romans 8:35, 37-39

These words are often read at funerals. In fact, I recently led a memorial service that included these verses. It's certainly appropriate to use these words to comfort the bereaved, but it seems to me that the rest of us can also benefit from reading and reflecting on them. We all face times of hardship, and during those times we may feel unloved and wonder if anyone really cares about us.

Some people turn away from God during difficult times. They conclude that a loving God would have intervened to prevent the tragic loss they are facing, and therefore God must not love them or perhaps does not exist at all. The woman whose memorial service I led became angry and bitter when her son died, and turned away from God. As I said at the service, though, that

5

doesn't mean that God turned away from her. These words remind us that NOTHING can separate us from the love of God. We are free to reject that love, but God continues to freely give it.

Other people desperately cling to God's love and depend on it to get through tough times. When I was in high school, I was not very popular. In fact, I frequently had closer friendships with my teachers than my peers! It was rare for me to have a date, much less a steady boyfriend. Somehow, though, I knew that God loved me. My family vacationed at the beach in Florida every summer, and airbrushed T-shirts with beach scenes were very popular at that time. I got the airbrush artist to do a different design for me, though: a cross with a dove and the words "God loves you no matter what." I cherished that T-shirt and kept it for many years; it was a tangible reminder that no matter how alone I felt, God loved me and would always be there for me.

Thankfully, I've also had people in my life to be "God with skin on" for me. My pastor when I was in high school, along with his wife, who was my English teacher, have been great sources of support and encouragement, along with the campus pastor of the college I attended, and plenty of other people God has brought into my life at various points along the way. I hope that the same is true for you.

Questions for Personal Reflection

1. Do you tend to draw closer to God or push God away during your times of hardship and distress?

2. Do you believe that God loves you? Do you have something tangible to remind you of that love?

3. Who is "God with skin on" for you?

"My God, my God, why have you forsaken me? Why are you so far from helping me, from the words of my groaning? O my God, I cry by day, but you do not answer; and by night, but find no rest. Do not be far from me, for trouble is near and there is no one to help."

Psalm 22:1-2, 11

At first glance, there may not seem to be anything comforting or hopeful in these words. The writer clearly feels abandoned by God, and wonders why God isn't answering his cries for help. Neither is anyone else. What's encouraging about that?

I included these verses because there have been times in my life when I have felt helpless and hopeless, so much so that I contemplated suicide. I have also counseled others who feel abandoned by God (and sometimes by friends and family, too).

What I have experienced myself and also heard from others is that the belief that God has forgotten us, or doesn't care that we are suffering, is often accompanied by feelings of guilt for doubting God, or being angry at God. We decide that we must be terrible people to feel that way, that we have no right to question God, and that because of our lack of faith, God has good reason to ignore our cries for help and we deserve to suffer.

That is why I believe the words of Psalm 22 are ultimately words of comfort and hope. Here we see that we are not the only ones to feel abandoned by God at times. This is one of many places in the Bible where people demand to know why God seems to have forgotten them or to be actively persecuting them. They don't hesitate to bring their grievances to God, and neither should we.

I had a theology professor in college who told us we shouldn't hesitate to get angry at God, and express that anger, because God can handle our anger better than anyone else can. There's a lot of wisdom in that. God knows what is in our hearts anyway, and any close relationship requires honest communication. God wants us to share everything, not just carefully thought out words that we think God wants to hear!

The other reason I like these verses is that despite feeling abandoned by God, the writer continues to ask God for help. Instead of saying to God, in effect, "You didn't give me what I asked for, so I'm through with you," he vents his frustration and feelings of abandonment but still begs God to draw closer to him in his time of need. We can all learn from that model!

Finally, as I mentioned in the introduction, Jesus himself uttered the words, "My God, my God, why have you forsaken me?" as he hung from the cross. Not only do we have a God who can handle our feelings of anger and despair, we have a God who has personally experienced them! Our God is not a far off God, emotionally detached from our struggles, but a loving, personal God who can fully relate to our feelings because he has felt them himself. What could be more comforting than that?

Questions for Personal Reflection

1. What does it mean to you to know that God has experienced great despair and feelings of abandonment?

2. Do you ever get angry at God, or feel abandoned by God? If so, do you express those feelings to God? How does God respond?

"The Lord is my shepherd; I shall not want.
He makes me lie down in green pastures;
he leads me beside still waters; he restores my soul.
He leads me in right paths for his name's sake.
Even though I walk through the darkest valley,
I fear no evil; for you are with me; your rod and your
staff—they comfort me."

Psalm 23:1-4

These words are among the most familiar and beloved words in all of Scripture (although the phrasing is slightly different in earlier translations: "paths of righteousness" instead of "right paths" and "valley of the shadow of death" instead of "the darkest valley"). When meeting with family members to plan a funeral or memorial service, I have heard more requests for Psalm 23 than for any other reading. It is a perennial favorite.

Why are so many people drawn to these words? I think it is because the imagery used is so soothing. In times of great upheaval in our lives, when the future we envisioned isn't working out as planned and we don't know what will happen to us, it is calming to hear of green pastures and still waters. We long for someone to lead us in right paths and restore our souls.

These days, most of us do not get to spend much time in green pastures or beside still waters. The hectic pace of daily life leaves little time for pausing to marvel at the beauty of nature, and there are fewer pristine wilderness areas left to admire anyway, as those areas are increasingly being built up or mined for natural resources to meet the demands of a growing population. Despite those realities, though, many people say they feel closest to God when they are out enjoying the wonders of God's creation, and find ways to do so, from taking a walk around the block to planning a vacation that includes hiking, camping, swimming, diving, skiing, or visiting a National Park or some other scenic area.

As wonderful as it is to enjoy the beauty of nature, though, there are times when that beauty can be dangerous. Hikers sometimes get lost and have to be rescued, campers may encounter bears or other animals that could pose a threat to them, and even a simple walk around the block can mean getting stung by an insect or tripping and falling. All of these activities are safer and more enjoyable when we have a trusted companion with us, especially if that person is familiar with the surroundings.

This Psalm reminds us that whether we are exploring a wilderness area or just trying to navigate the ever-changing terrain of our life's journey, we have a shepherd to guide us, one who knows the way when we are lost and comforts us along the way. That shepherd is none other than the very one who created us and continues to sustain us throughout our lives. When we walk through the darkest valleys of our lives, we can rest assured that we have nothing to fear, because we do not walk alone.

Questions for Personal Reflection

1. How does God restore your soul? If you cannot literally lie down in green pastures or rest beside still waters, is there someplace you can go (either physically or in your imagination) to lay your burdens down, relax, and rest in God's loving embrace?

2. Is there a "right path" on which God is leading you? If so, are you going willingly or resisting every step of the way? Is God in front of you, beside you, or pushing you from behind?

"He (Jesus) said to him, 'You shall love the Lord your God with all your heart, and with all your soul, and with all your mind.' This is the greatest and first commandment. And a second is like it: 'You shall love your neighbor as yourself.' On these two commandments hang all the law and the prophets."

Matthew 22:37-40

Jesus himself says that these are the most important commandments, so they are well worth a closer look. First, we are told to love the Lord with all of our heart, soul, and mind. In other words, God wants a total commitment, the complete devotion of our entire being.

What does that mean? It means that we use our minds to learn about God, to study God's word and church teachings, and think about what we believe and why. We open our hearts to God, and talk *with* God instead of just *about* God. We express praise and adoration, confess our sins, show our gratitude for all that God has done for us, bring our concerns to God, and honestly share whatever we are feeling. We bare our souls, the very essence of who we are, before God and allow God to use our unique talents and personalities in a way that glorifies God and benefits others.

Next, we are told, "Love your neighbor as yourself." In other words, treat other people with respect, speak the truth in love, and care about their needs as much as you care about your own. Recognize the face of God in every person you encounter, and in the mirror, because we are all created in God's image, and we are all God's beloved children.

The second part of that commandment is equally important – to love ourselves. Note that we are not told to love our neighbor more than ourselves, but as ourselves. I don't know about you, but I sometimes find it easier to love my neighbor than to love myself! I am harder on myself than anyone else, and have a relentless inner critic telling me what I did wrong or what I should have accomplished but didn't. It's an ongoing struggle to truly love myself unconditionally, the way that God loves me and calls me to love myself and others.

Just imagine what the world would be like if each of us loved God with all of our heart, soul, and mind, and loved our neighbors as ourselves. Decisions would be made based on the common good, those in need of food or shelter would encounter people who have more than enough and are happy to share with them, there would be no crime, kids would not get bullied at school…the list could go on and on. While we are not likely to experience the full realization of that vision during our time on Earth, we can move closer to it by seeking to live according to these two commandments regardless of what others do. There are numerous examples of individuals who have shown that one person can indeed make a difference, and inspire others to go and do likewise.

Questions for Personal Reflection

1. What does it mean to you to love God with all your heart, soul, and mind? How do you express your love for God?

2. Is it harder for you to love your neighbor or to love yourself? How do you show your love for others, and for yourself?

"Rejoice in the Lord always; again I will say, Rejoice. Let your gentleness be known to everyone. The Lord is near. Do not worry about anything, but in everything by prayer and supplication with thanksgiving let your requests be made known to God. And the peace of God, which surpasses all understanding, will guard your hearts and your minds in Christ Jesus."

Philippians 4:4-7

It sounds so simple, doesn't it? Rejoice, the Lord is near, don't worry about anything, just pray and be filled with God's peace. On the one hand, it *is* simple, and I am grateful for the times that I am able to do that and trust that somehow everything will work out.

On the other hand, though, it is unbelievably difficult to rejoice when times are tough; more often than not I *do* worry, and I know plenty of others who are worried, too. We believe in God, and know that God will ultimately save us, but we'd really like God to share more details of the plan with us, so we can have some idea of exactly how and when our prayers will be answered!

The peace of God can seem far away when we are wondering how we will pay the bills, or cope with a loved one's illness or death, or overcome an addiction, or find meaningful work, or heal from a broken heart, or otherwise make it through another day. As much as we might like to have God's peace guarding our hearts and minds, we often find our hearts filled with anger, fear and sorrow instead of joy, and our minds dwelling on our problems instead of how God can work in and through us to solve those problems.

These verses are both a promise and a challenge. The promise is that God is near, and will give us a peace that surpasses all understanding. The challenge is that we are called to rejoice even when we aren't feeling very happy, and let our requests be made known to God even when it seems like God isn't listening, or at least isn't responding in the way that we were expecting.

I find it interesting that so many self-help books tell us to think about what we want and therefore somehow magically attract it, and to keep gratitude journals so we focus on what we have and are thankful for, instead of what we lack. These verses suggest something very similar, but with a key difference: instead of relying on our own efforts alone, we turn to a God who knows us even better than we know ourselves, has abilities and resources far beyond our own, and acts to save us even when we aren't sure that is possible or that we're worth saving. God's presence in our lives gives us good reason to rejoice, no matter what we are facing, and to be at peace.

Questions for Personal Reflection

1. Do you believe that the Lord is near to you? If not, how can you draw closer to God?

2. Do you include thanksgiving when you are making your requests known to God? For what are you most thankful?

3. How do you understand the peace of God? In what ways have you experienced that peace in your life?

"Have you not known? Have you not heard? The Lord is the everlasting God, the Creator of the ends of the earth. He does not faint or grow weary; his understanding is unsearchable. He gives power to the faint, and strengthens the powerless. Even youths will faint and be weary, and the young will fall exhausted; but those who wait for the Lord shall renew their strength, they shall mount up with wings like eagles, they shall run and not be weary, they shall walk and not faint."

Isaiah 40:28-31

At first, I laughed when I read these verses, because I thought back to the many lock-ins and overnight trips with youth that I chaperoned as a youth director and later as a pastor, and remembered how late at night I often wished the youths would be weary and fall exhausted, but that rarely happened! Some of them were weary in another sense, though: emotionally weary as they dealt with their parents' marriages ending and shuttling back and forth between two different households with different rules, or being bullied at school, or seeing their former boyfriend or girlfriend with someone else, or an addiction to drugs or alcohol, or an unplanned pregnancy. They were weary from being pressured to do things that they knew were wrong, and from trying desperately to fit in with the crowd.

As adults, we are often weary too, aren't we? Whether it's physical exhaustion from working long hours, parenting children, and/or caring for an aging relative, or mental exhaustion from worrying about our financial situation, a strained relationship, a loved one's illness, or any of a host of other challenges we face in our daily lives, we know what it is to be weary.

And yet we persevere. With God's help, we keep going and find ways to renew our strength and "mount up with wings like eagles." Have you ever seen an eagle in flight? What I've noticed is that it is rare to see them flapping their wings; they seem to soar effortlessly for incredibly long distances. God enables us to do the same.

These verses remind us that we don't have to rely on our efforts alone; it is God who strengthens us and gives us power when we are faint and feel powerless. Certainly, we have to do our part, but when we don't think we can go on, we have a God who does not faint or grow weary, and who shows us how to renew our strength and continue our life's journey, come what may.

Questions for Personal Reflection

1. What wearies you? How do you deal with that weariness?

2. Have you ever felt strengthened or empowered by God to do something you did not think you could do?

3. What does "wait for the Lord" mean to you? How do you do that?

"For whatever was written in former days was written for our encouragement, so that by steadfastness and by the encouragement of the scriptures we might have hope. May the God of steadfastness and encouragement grant you to live in harmony with one another, in accordance with Christ Jesus, so that together you may with one voice glorify the God and Father of our Lord Jesus Christ. May the God of hope fill you with all joy and peace in believing, so that you may abound in hope by the power of the Holy Spirit."

Romans 15:4-5, 13

These words were written to the church in Rome, at a time when that church was quarreling over things like whether or not to pay taxes to the Roman government (and otherwise be subject to its authority) and whether or not it was okay to eat meat. Even way back then, there were church disagreements that sometimes caused divisions. The issues may be different today, but arguments about what the church should teach or how things should be done have been a reality for thousands of years, from the very beginning of the church's existence!

Paul knows that the people need to be reminded of what is most important, so he writes a letter stating the need for them to live in harmony with one another, and respect each other's opinions instead of fighting over who is right. This is not just for their own benefit, he argues, but so that together they can glorify God. Wouldn't it be nice if individual congregations, denominations, and Christians throughout the world could do that?

Paul tells us that it is possible, but not through human effort alone. It is God who enables us to live in harmony despite our diverse opinions. God gives us scriptures to instruct and encourage us, and fills us with joy and peace. God's Holy Spirit empowers us to abound with hope in the midst of conflict.

The words "steadfastness" and "encouragement" are used repeatedly in these verses. We are told that we might have hope "by steadfastness and by the encouragement of the scriptures," and God is referred to as "the God of steadfastness and encouragement." Both qualities are essential. Steadfastness keeps us faithful when we are tempted to give up on the church (or on God), and keeps us determined to try to have conversations with and better understand people with whom we disagree, so that we can find ways to work together for God's glory. Encouragement lifts us up when we find it hard to remain hopeful, and emboldens us to speak the truth in love and make needed changes when the church has forgotten or neglected its mission. Both are gifts God gives us for the building up of the body of Christ.

Questions for Personal Reflection

1. Are there particular issues that are causing dissension at your church? If so, how can you address those issues in a healthy way?

2. If you do not attend church right now, is that because you left over a specific controversy about a church teaching or action, or otherwise had a negative church experience at some point? Are you happy with your choice not to attend, or would you like to be active in a church?

3. Does God currently "fill you with all joy and peace in believing, so that you may abound in hope?" If not, what is preventing you from experiencing that joy and peace?

"Therefore walk in the way of the good, and keep to the paths of the just. For the upright will abide in the land, and the innocent will remain in it; but the wicked will be cut off from the land, and the treacherous will be rooted out of it. My child, do not forget my teaching, but let your heart keep my commandments; for length of days and years of life and abundant welfare they will give you."

Proverbs 2:20-3:2

Lately, it has increasingly seemed like it is the wicked who abide in the land and have abundant welfare. The treacherous seem to prosper while the innocent suffer. It is easy to lose hope, and to dismiss these verses as naïve and idealistic.

The reality is that God's teachings do indeed give us "years of life and abundant welfare" when we follow them. The abundant welfare does not necessarily mean wealth or material possessions, though; it is well-being in a far deeper sense. Have you ever noticed that it is often people who live in the poorest countries and have the least that are the most joyful, will walk miles and then stand for hours to worship and praise God together, and who generously share what little they do have? They often struggle to survive, and yet they manage to be happy. Meanwhile, there are many Hollywood celebrities and professional athletes who have tons of money (and houses, and cars, and all of the other things that money can buy), yet have been divorced multiple times, are addicted to drugs or alcohol, or are otherwise miserable despite their riches.

Of course, that is a generalization; I do realize that there are plenty of poor people who are not joy-filled and eager to praise God, just as there are rich people who are happily married and use their wealth to do a lot of good in the world. I also realize that all of us, at times, forget God's teachings, stray from the path of the just, and fail to walk in the way of the good. It is too easy to point fingers and find scapegoats to blame for the world's problems, and to see ourselves as innocent victims.

One thing that is very clear throughout the Bible is that we are all both saints and sinners. Many people mentioned in the Bible, even the great heroes like Moses and David and Paul, do terrible things, including murdering people and committing adultery. The people of Israel repeatedly turn away from God to worship other gods, disobey God's commandments, and infuriate God to the point that Israel "received from the Lord's hand double for all her sins." (Isaiah 40:2)

There is an endless cycle: the people ignore God and reject God's teachings, do whatever they feel like doing, stop providing for widows and orphans and others in need, adopt the practices of the culture around them to the point that those who believe in God are indistinguishable from those who don't, notice that their way of living isn't working anymore, angrily cry out to God for help and wonder why God doesn't seem to be listening. Sooner or later the people recognize their sin, repent, and turn back to God. God acts to save them, things are great for a time, then the people start ignoring God's teachings and the cycle starts again.

The good news is that God never tires of forgiving, and acts over and over again to rescue us. The bad news is that it often takes a lot of suffering before we realize the error of our ways and are willing to once again "walk in the way of the good, and keep to the paths of the just."

Questions for Personal Reflection

1. In what ways are you currently walking in the way of the good? In what ways are you acting wicked or treacherous?

2. How do you remember God's teachings? Which teachings of God would you prefer to forget?

3. How have you experienced years of life and abundant welfare by keeping God's commandments in your heart?

"Therefore do not worry, saying 'What will we eat?' or 'What will we drink?' or 'What will we wear?' For it is the Gentiles who strive for all these things; and indeed your heavenly Father knows that you need all these things. But strive first for the kingdom of God and its righteousness, and all these things will be given to you as well. So do not worry about tomorrow, for tomorrow will bring worries of its own. Today's trouble is enough for today."

Matthew 6:31-34

God knows what we need and will provide it, so there's no reason to worry. Sounds great, doesn't it? However, there are a lot of people who don't have food to eat or water that is safe to drink. Children die of starvation every day, and even in wealthy countries like the U.S. there are people who go hungry. How can we not worry? Should we just close our eyes to the world's problems and pretend that everything is fine?

I think these verses tell us to do just the opposite. They remind us that when we strive first for the kingdom of God and its righteousness, then we will also get our basic needs for food, drink, and clothing met. It is when we hoard more than we need, steal resources that are not ours, and refuse to share with others who have less than we do, that problems arise.

These verses also tell us not to worry about *tomorrow.* In other words, live in the present moment and focus on the challenges we are facing *now,* not the problems that we fear we may have to face later. Perhaps you've heard that 95% of what we worry about never actually happens. I couldn't find the original source of that often quoted statistic, so I can't verify its accuracy, but I know in my own life I have worried about many things that never actually happened to me, even though I was convinced they were inevitable outcomes and wasted a lot of time and energy worrying about them.

The most destructive thing about worry is that it can paralyze us, and actually keep us from taking concrete actions to address the real difficulties we are facing. We spend our time dwelling on what *could* happen, and convince ourselves that our situation is only going to get worse so there's no point in trying to improve it because it's hopeless. Jesus himself points out that worrying is useless when he asks, "Can any of you, by worrying, add a single hour to your span of life?" (Matthew 6:27)

Ultimately, the future is in God's hands, and when we strive first for the kingdom of God and its righteousness, God is able to work in and through us to help make that future brighter.

Questions for Personal Reflection

1. What are your current worries?

2. What have you worried about in the past that never happened? If you have worried about something that *did* happen, did worrying about it help in any way?

3. What does it mean to you to "strive first for the kingdom of God and its righteousness?" How can you do that in your everyday life?

"For everything there is a season, and a time for every purpose under heaven: a time to be born, and a time to die; a time to plant, and a time to pluck up what is planted; a time to kill, and a time to heal; a time to break down, and a time to build up; a time to weep, and a time to laugh; a time to mourn, and a time to dance."

Ecclesiastes 3:1-4

The book of Ecclesiastes is an interesting book. On the one hand, the author seems to be saying that all of our efforts are pointless, that the same fate befalls the wicked and the righteous, and that it is impossible to understand the meaning of life or God's plan for us, "for who knows what is good for mortals while they live the few days of their vain life, which they pass like a shadow?" (Ecclesiastes 6:12) Not exactly words of comfort and hope, and not a book I would recommend to someone who is already in despair and unable to imagine a better future!

On the other hand, there are pearls of wisdom scattered throughout the book, like the verses quoted above, and it does emphasize enjoying life despite its struggles and trusting that God is in control even when we can't figure out why things are the way they are. The book ends with the advice to "fear God, and keep his commandments; for that is the whole duty of everyone." (Ecclesiastes 12:13) That sounds like good advice to me!

I love these verses because they remind me that life has an innate rhythm, a flow that goes on and brings a variety of people and situations to each of us. Some of those people and situations we might wish we had not encountered, and yet we learn and grow from all of them. They are usually necessary for some reason, even though we may not understand it at the time (or, in some cases, ever).

Just as a woman must go through the pain of childbirth to experience the joy of holding her newborn child, we must each go through times of weeping and mourning in order to bring about or be able to fully appreciate the times of laughter and dancing. We have to plant, and nurture what we plant, before it will grow into something worth plucking up. We have to break down before we can build up, whether we are remodeling a house, ending a destructive relationship (or working to transform it into one worth saving), overcoming an addiction, or embarking on a new venture. Something has to die to make room for something new to be born.

These verses help us picture the larger tapestry of our lives when we are seeing only a particular thread that we don't like. They give us courage to keep moving forward, as hard as it is sometimes, and to trust that whatever is happening now, our current season of life is temporary. Just as the barrenness of winter always gives way to the new life of spring, our troubled times always give way to new possibilities.

Questions for Personal Reflection

1. What season is it in your life? What is it time for you to do?

2. Is there something or someone you need to let go of to prepare to enter the next season of your life?

3. Do you believe that God controls what happens to us? Why or why not? What is our role in shaping our future, and what is God's?

"On that day, when evening had come, he (Jesus) said to them, 'Let us go across to the other side.' And leaving the crowd behind, they took him with them in the boat, just as he was. Other boats were with him. A great windstorm arose, and the waves beat into the boat, so that the boat was already being swamped. But he was in the stern, asleep on the cushion; and they woke him up and said to him, 'Teacher, do you not care that we are perishing?' He woke up and rebuked the wind, and said to the sea, 'Peace! Be still!' Then the wind ceased, and there was a dead calm. He said to them, 'Why are you afraid? Have you still no faith?'"

Mark 4:35-40

Have you ever been on a boat during stormy conditions, when the wind is fierce and the waves are splashing into the boat? I have, and it can be a frightening experience. As much as I normally enjoy being out on a boat, I still remember one rough ferry crossing at night when I was a child during which I was very afraid we might not make it to the other side.

Even if you've never experienced it personally, chances are you can imagine what it would be like to be on a boat, at night, during a storm. It certainly would not be a peaceful, relaxing experience. Do you think there is any way you could *sleep* in those conditions?

Somehow, Jesus does manage to sleep while the boat is being swamped by waves. The terrified disciples wake him up and ask him if he cares that they are dying, he commands the wind and the sea to be still, and suddenly there is a dead calm. Jesus then asks his companions why they are afraid and even goes so far as to say, "Have you still no faith?"

I love this story for several reasons. First, the fact that Jesus is able to sleep in the midst of the storm. That shows a level of relaxation and complete trust in God that I wish I had in the midst of storms in my life. Second, because Jesus takes charge, rebuking the wind and telling the sea, in effect, "Stop that this instant!" and they obey without question. I wish that every time Jesus uttered the command, "Peace! Be still!" to me, I would immediately calm down and do whatever else Jesus tells me to do without questioning it or complaining.

Most of all, though, I love this story because of Jesus' question to the disciples, "Have you still no faith?" This story is one of many instances in the Bible, and especially in the Gospel of Mark, where the disciples just don't get it. They don't understand who Jesus is, how he is able to do what he does, what they're supposed to do, or why things that they don't like, especially Jesus' arrest and crucifixion, have to happen. Despite the many ways in which they disappoint Jesus and even betray him, though, he continues to love them and uses them to proclaim his message.

Jesus' confidence in the disciples, and his willingness to forgive them when they fall short of his hopes for them, is comforting because all of us, at times, lack faith or fail to do what God asks of us. We can rest assured that we are loved and forgiven, just as the first disciples were.

Questions for Personal Reflection

1. Are there times in your life when God seems to be asleep and unconcerned that you are suffering? What do you do to get God's attention?

2. Do you tend to lack faith during stormy periods in your life? How do you strengthen your faith? How does God act to save you despite your fears and doubts?

3. How does God use you to proclaim God's message? In what ways does your life show the power of God's love and forgiveness?

"But this I call to mind, and therefore I have hope: The steadfast love of the Lord never ceases, his mercies never come to an end; they are new every morning; great is your faithfulness. 'The Lord is my portion,' says my soul, 'therefore I will hope in him.' The Lord is good to those who wait for him, to the soul that seeks him. It is good that one should wait quietly for the salvation of the Lord."

Lamentations 3:21-26

I don't wait well. When I want something, I want it NOW, and if there is a long line at a store or restaurant I usually decide it's not worth the wait and leave. I have learned over the course of my life, though, that there are some things worth the wait, and also that acting on my desire for instant gratification sometimes causes me to do something I later regret, or keeps me from being able to get something better later.

The author of Lamentations has also apparently learned the value of waiting, at least when it comes to God's salvation. What I find remarkable is that in all of the verses leading up to the ones quoted here, the writer expresses great despair over the destruction of Zion. He blames God for all of the terrible things that have happened (though ultimately he blames the people, himself included, because their sin provoked God's wrath), says God has shut out his prayers, torn him to pieces, and left him desolate, and concludes, "The thought of my affliction and my homelessness is wormwood and gall! My soul continually thinks of it and is bowed down within me." (Lamentations 3:19-20).

Immediately after that statement, though, he says the steadfast love of the Lord never ceases and that it is good to wait quietly for the salvation of the Lord! I find that attitude remarkable, given all that has happened to him. Somehow, he holds on to the belief that God is good, and that better days are coming, despite the death and destruction he sees all around him. He goes on to challenge others to do the same, saying, "Let us test and examine our ways, and return to the Lord. Let us lift up our hearts as well as our hands to God in heaven." (Lamentations 3:40-41)

Not only do I think the author of Lamentations is a wonderful example of someone who trusts God's love and faithfulness in the midst of very troubled times, I also think he provides an excellent model for communication with others when our relationship with them is strained. First, the author pleads his case directly to God, instead of complaining to someone else about how God has wronged him. He doesn't make threats, or stop talking to God, or plot revenge because he is hurt and angry. Next, after clearly stating his grievances, he acknowledges his own role in the problem and expresses regret for his past actions. Finally, he makes it clear that he still believes in God's goodness, knows that God loves him, and has hope because of that. I suspect that many marriages, friendships, and other human relationships could be saved if we all consistently communicated that way!

Questions for Personal Reflection

1. What does it mean to seek the Lord, and to wait quietly for the salvation of the Lord? How do you do that?

2. Do you believe that God causes us to suffer as punishment for our sins? Why or why not?

3. Is there someone with whom you have a strained relationship? If so, do you think using the communication method mentioned above could improve that relationship? Are you willing to try it?

"Come to me, all you that are weary and are carrying heavy burdens, and I will give you rest. Take my yoke upon you, and learn from me; for I am gentle and humble in heart, and you will find rest for your souls. For my yoke is easy, and my burden is light."

Matthew 11:28-30

Just reading those words calms me. We are all weary at times, aren't we? I also don't know anyone who isn't carrying a heavy burden of some kind. Even when our own lives are going great, there is almost always a friend or family member who is not doing so well that worries us. Jesus promises rest, and invites us to take his yoke and learn from him, because his yoke is easy and his burden is light.

Wait a minute; how can he say that his burden is light? He is rejected in his hometown, his cousin John is beheaded, his disciples betray him, and he is mocked, beaten, and dies in agony on a cross. That certainly doesn't sound like a light burden to me! In fact, my own burdens don't seem heavy at all in comparison to his.

These words clearly aren't a guarantee that once we come to Jesus, life will be carefree and nothing bad will ever happen to us again. Plenty of bad things happened to Jesus himself. What is being promised is actually far greater: rest for our souls even in the midst of the most trying times imaginable.

Jesus can say that his yoke is easy and his burden is light because he knows he doesn't have to carry it alone. He prays often; on the night of his arrest alone, he leaves his disciples and goes off to pray three different times. He knows that his life is in God's hands and therefore everything will ultimately work out.

Jesus invites us to learn from him. Through his teachings, and even more so through the example of his own life, we learn what it means to truly love God, our neighbors, and ourselves. We learn how to be gentle and humble in heart. Most of all, we learn that even the heaviest burden is light when we place it in God's hands.

Questions for Personal Reflection

1. What are the heavy burdens that you are carrying?

2. How does Jesus give you rest?

3. What do you need to learn from Jesus?

"I lift up my eyes to the hills – from where will my help come? My help comes from the Lord, who made heaven and earth. He will not let your foot be moved; he who keeps you will not slumber."

Psalm 121:1-3

I read a lot of fiction, especially thrillers in which the police or private investigators are in hot pursuit of a serial killer. In many of these novels, the killer captures the person he intends to be his next victim (often the hero or heroine of the story, who has been trying to stop him from hurting anyone else) and starts gleefully making preparations to maximize the suffering he will inflict. During this time, the would-be victim is kept hidden in a secret location, in restraints and under guard. The situation seems hopeless until he or she finds a way to escape, almost always by either waiting until the guard falls asleep naturally or forcing that to happen by drugging him or knocking him unconscious.

I mention that because one of the characteristics of God mentioned in this Psalm is that God does not sleep. God is awake all of the time, not to prevent our escape but to lovingly watch over us and hear us when we cry for help. While it may seem like God has fallen asleep when our prayers don't get answered in the way or the time frame that we have in mind, the reality is that God is always present and aware of what is happening. Whether our help comes in the form of a miraculous rescue, a wise friend or counselor, a medical professional, or even death as a blessed release from our suffering, it ultimately comes from God.

One of the most common misconceptions people have is that the Bible says, "God helps those who help themselves." That phrase is not actually in the Bible at all; in fact, there are numerous Bible verses that say just the opposite, emphasizing that God intervenes to help those who are helpless and that we are saved by grace, not because we did something to deserve it. Of course, that doesn't mean we should sit back and do nothing when we are capable of helping ourselves; the point is that when we cannot, God can and will act. Our help does indeed come from the Lord, who made heaven and earth, and who made each of us and lovingly watches over us.

Questions for Personal Reflection

1. Do you believe that God watches over you without sleeping? Is that thought comforting or frightening to you?

2. How has God acted to help you in the past? Is there a particular situation in your life now that you need God's help to handle?

"May you be made strong with all the strength that comes from his glorious power, and may you be prepared to endure everything with patience, while joyfully giving thanks to the Father, who has enabled you to share in the inheritance of the saints in the light. He has rescued us from the power of darkness and transferred us into the kingdom of his beloved Son, in whom we have redemption, the forgiveness of sins."

Colossians 1:11-14

"God, give me strength." I have heard others say that on numerous occasions, and I have prayed it myself, both when I have been called to minister with people in tragic situations and when I have faced my own troubled times. It is a cry for help, a recognition that we don't feel up to dealing with what is happening to us.

Somehow, God does give us the strength to make it through difficult times. I still remember vividly the days following September 11, 2011. I was in shock, angry, and fearful after the terrorist attacks. My brother's office was only a few blocks from the World Trade Center; thankfully he was safe, but I spent several anxious hours waiting to find out. I was pastor of a church in Pennsylvania at the time, so I needed to prepare a sermon for that Sunday.

What could I say that would give people hope in the face of such a great tragedy? God gave me the strength to boldly proclaim the gospel and challenge the mindset of those who were eager to retaliate and didn't care how many innocent civilians were killed in the process. God also led me to start a weekly gathering at the church so that we could honestly share our thoughts and feelings about everything that was happening in the aftermath of the attacks and then pray together.

In addition to wishing us strength, the writer of these verses also wishes for us to be prepared to endure everything with patience, while joyfully giving thanks to the Father. That is asking a lot! It's hard to joyfully give thanks while enduring great difficulties. One of the most powerful examples of someone who was able to do that is a woman in New Orleans after Hurricane Katrina. The youth group of Kihei Lutheran Church, the church I attend on Maui, went there on a mission trip, and helped gut this woman's house down to the studs, since it was full of mold after being flooded. The homeowner was standing on her front lawn, surrounded by the few possessions she had been able to salvage, yet when asked how she was, she responded, "I am blessed." She meant it, too; she was genuinely thankful to God that she had survived and that people were helping her.

May God give each of us strength, patience, and the ability to joyfully give thanks even in the midst of our most challenging times.

Questions for Personal Reflection

1. How does God strengthen you? How has God rescued you from the power of darkness?

2. Do you joyfully give thanks to God? For what are you most grateful?

3. How do you know when it is appropriate to endure everything with patience, and when it is time to end a destructive relationship, find a new job, or otherwise make a major change in your life?

"There are many who say, 'O that we might see some good! Let the light of your face shine on us, O Lord!' You have put gladness in my heart, more than when their grain and wine abound. I will both lie down and sleep in peace, for you alone, O Lord, make me lie down in safety."

Psalm 4:6-8

Who wouldn't like to see some good? Television news anchors are quick to tell us about the latest murders, rapes, car accidents, natural disasters, wars, and other catastrophic events. At best, we get a token feel good story included with all of the bad news. It is hard to see the positive when we keep hearing about all that is wrong with the world.

God can indeed put gladness in our hearts, though, even in the midst of our most trying times. I know this because I have experienced it. As I write this, my husband and I are both unemployed and, just in the last month or so, our car has leaked engine coolant and required a new water pump, we have had to replace the water heater in our condo, and our cat is in the animal hospital with a temporary feeding tube in her neck. Lately it seems like every time I wonder what else could possibly go wrong, something else does!

However, in some ways I am happier than I've been in a long time. As I continue to look for work, I have also been able to use this unexpected time off to volunteer at our church's afterschool program, write this book, take walks on the beach, and otherwise do things that I enjoy. I have drawn closer to God, and find myself praying and reading the Bible more often. I have discovered that when I look for good news, I can always find some.

Most of all, I have recognized the reality that it is indeed God alone who can provide true safety and security. I used to think my security came from a steady paycheck, but now that I've been let go from two different companies in the last few years, as each decided to save money by eliminating my position, I know that job security is an illusion. I also know that what is truly important in life can't be taken away when I can no longer afford to pay for it.

Because of that, I can sleep in peace. My life has taken some unexpected turns; yours probably has too. We may not know what the future holds for us, but we know that God is with us every step of the way, and that alone is reason for our hearts to be filled with gladness!

Questions for Personal Reflection

1. What do you see that is good in your life, in your community, and in the wider world?

2. Has God put gladness in your heart? If not, have you asked God for that gift? Is there something you especially enjoy that you could do to feel glad even when times are tough?

3. Do you feel safe? Why or why not? How does God help you lie down and sleep in peace?

"And Mary said, 'My soul magnifies the Lord, and my spirit rejoices in God my Savior, for he has looked with favor on the lowliness of his servant. Surely, from now on all generations will call me blessed; for the Mighty One has done great things for me, and holy is his name. His mercy is for those who fear him from generation to generation.'"

Luke 1:46-50

Mary's faith has always amazed and inspired me. When the angel Gabriel visits her and announces that she will bear a son and name him Jesus, she doesn't say, "No way; you've got the wrong girl," as I suspect many young girls would. She simply asks how this will happen, since she is a virgin, and when she is told that God's power will overshadow her and her child will be holy and called the Son of God, she replies, "Here am I, the servant of the Lord; let it be with me according to your word." (Luke 1:38)

I admire her willingness to agree so readily; I'm sure I would have had a few more questions and wanted to think about it before I gave my consent. I also think it's remarkable that she is so quick to praise God, rejoice, and declare confidently that from now on everyone will call her blessed. She doesn't express any concern about how Joseph will react to the fact that she is pregnant, or what her family and friends will think. She doesn't seem at all frightened by the prospect of labor pains or the challenges of parenthood.

Her trust in God is so complete that she expresses only gratitude that God has bestowed this honor upon her.

I would love to have the level of trust in God that Mary has! Even when I feel certain about what God has called me to do, I am frequently fearful. Instead of being grateful for the opportunity, I worry that I am not up to the challenge and will disappoint God and others. God often has to keep pushing me before I finally do what God wants me to do.

These verses are a good reminder to all of us that the best response when God intervenes in our lives in dramatic ways, or asks us to do something unexpected, is to be grateful and rejoice. We can celebrate that God has done great things not only for Mary, but for each of us, and we are all blessed.

Questions for Personal Reflection

1. In what ways are you blessed? What great things has God done for you?

2. How do you know when God wants you to do something? Is there anything you believe God is calling you to do currently that you have been resisting?

"The Lord is my light and my salvation; whom shall I fear? The Lord is the stronghold of my life; of whom shall I be afraid? I believe that I shall see the goodness of the Lord in the land of the living. Wait for the Lord; be strong, and let your heart take courage; wait for the Lord!"

Psalm 27:1, 13-14

It's easy to be afraid these days. We are constantly being warned about things like terrorist threats, dangerous criminals on the loose, storms headed our way, cancer-causing substances, economic problems, and even falling space debris. Of whom (or what) shall I be afraid? I can think of many possibilities!

Ultimately, though, the writer of these verses is right to remind us that we have nothing to fear. With God as our stronghold, no matter what happens to us, we are victorious in the end. Even if we are killed, we go on to eternal life with God.

These verses don't just point to the hope of life after death, though; the author makes that clear by stating, "I shall see the goodness of the Lord in the land of the living." What I have noticed in my own life is that I can choose to see the goodness of the Lord at any point. It is just as easy for me to find inspirational stories of miraculous rescues, or people who have overcome great obstacles and then helped others do the same, or of ordinary people showing kindness to someone in need, as it is to listen to news reports about all of the bad things happening in the world.

Have you heard of Nick Vujicic? If you have internet access, watch one of his videos on YouTube. Nick was born without any arms or legs, so you can imagine the challenges he has faced. At one point, tired of being teased by other kids at school, worried about being a lifelong burden to his parents, and unable to imagine a future worth living, he almost committed suicide. Today, he is a world famous motivational speaker and has done all kinds of things, including surfing and scuba diving, that would not seem possible given his lack of limbs. He has a strong faith in God, and his book, *Life Without Limits*, is a powerful reminder that with God all things are possible.

Nick is one of many people who have found the strength and courage to do remarkable things. May God help each of us do the same!

Questions for Personal Reflection

1. What are your fears? How does God help you overcome those fears?

2. Where do you see the goodness of the Lord?

3. How can you help others see God's goodness, be strong, and have courage?

"Therefore, since we are justified by faith, we have peace with God through our Lord Jesus Christ, through whom we have obtained access to this grace in which we stand; and we boast in our hope of sharing the glory of God. And not only that, but we also boast in our sufferings, knowing that suffering produces endurance, and endurance produces character, and character produces hope, and hope does not disappoint us, because God's love has been poured into our hearts through the Holy Spirit that has been given to us."

Romans 5:1-5

Paul, the author of Romans, knows a thing or two about suffering. He was imprisoned multiple times, survived an angry mob's attempt to stone him to death, and, after many harrowing days on stormy seas, the boat on which he was traveling as a prisoner en route to Rome ran aground and he had to swim to shore. When he writes about boasting in our sufferings, he is not making a philosophical argument based on general principles; he is reflecting on his own personal experiences of suffering.

Paul considered it an honor to suffer, because his suffering was the direct result of his decision to boldly proclaim Christ's resurrection, and thus it was proof of his faithfulness and cause for boasting. Most of us will not be imprisoned or have people trying to kill us when we share our faith, though. In fact, some of us may not suffer at all because of our faith, but we will all experience suffering in some way for a wide variety of other reasons, so we can still benefit from Paul's wisdom.

Paul goes on to say that suffering produces endurance, endurance produces character, and character produces hope. Even though I would much rather gain endurance, character, and hope some other way than through suffering, I have to admit that he is right. Almost everyone that I know who has been through tough times, myself included, has benefitted from those experiences in some way. Some have discovered an inner strength they didn't know they had; some have learned that it's okay to ask for help; some have found out just how much their family and friends care about them; some have developed a clearer sense of who they are, what really matters to them, and how they want to live; some have embarked on new careers or started non-profit organizations to share what they have learned and help others facing what they have gone through, and all have been changed in profound ways because of their suffering.

Finally, Paul reminds us that hope does not disappoint us, because God's love has been poured into our hearts. I love that image; I can actually envision a pitcher pouring God's love into our hearts until they are full. That empty void that we all feel at times, when we wonder if anyone really cares about us and if our lives really matter, is filled as only God can fill it, with an unconditional love that never ends.

Questions for Personal Reflection

1. Have you been through times of suffering that produced endurance, character, and/or hope? How have your tough times changed you?

2. How do you experience God's love being poured into your heart? How does that love make a difference in your life? How do you share that love with others?

"Make me to know your ways, O Lord; teach me your paths. Lead me in your truth, and teach me, for you are the God of my salvation; for you I wait all day long. Be mindful of your mercy, O Lord, and of your steadfast love, for they have been from of old. Do not remember the sins of my youth or my transgressions; according to your steadfast love remember me, for your goodness' sake, O Lord!"

Psalm 25:4-7

There are many paths we can take in life, and we all make some wrong turns along the way. Sometimes we make what seems like a good decision at the time, and then realize later that we've made a mistake; at other times we give in to temptation and do something that we know is wrong. Either way, our actions have consequences that we have to face.

The writer of this Psalm asks God to make him know God's ways, to teach him God's paths, and lead him in God's truth. I would guess you've probably prayed for similar guidance; I certainly have. Occasionally, God makes it very clear to me what path I'm supposed to take, but most of the time I get only a vague sense of the direction in which I'm supposed to head, and am not sure what the actual destination is, how long it will take to reach it, or exactly how to get there. Over and over again, I learn that I have to let God lead me, and show me the way as we go.

When I don't follow God's guidance, I tend to be very hard on myself. I still feel guilty for things I said and did as a teenager, and seem to think that somehow during my teen years I should have had the wisdom and maturity to make the choices I would make now if I had it all to do over again. Since many of the church members who came to me for pastoral counseling were also wrestling with guilt and shame over something from their past, I know these regrets are common.

Although some of us have a hard time forgiving ourselves, the good news is that God is always willing to forgive us. God truly does not remember our transgressions, and is eager to lovingly lead us back to God's truth and teach us God's ways. We have a merciful God whose steadfast love sustains us even when we find it difficult to love ourselves.

Questions for Personal Reflection

1. How has God taught you which paths to take in life, and led you in God's truth?

2. When have you strayed from God's ways? How have God's mercy and steadfast love helped you face the consequences of those actions and find your way back to God's paths?

"I have said these things to you while I am still with you. But the Advocate, the Holy Spirit, whom the Father will send in my name, will teach you everything, and remind you of all that I have said to you. Peace I leave with you; my peace I give to you. I do not give to you as the world gives. Do not let your hearts be troubled, and do not let them be afraid."

John 14:25-27

Jesus speaks these words to his disciples immediately after telling them that he won't be with them much longer, that Judas will betray him, and that Peter will deny knowing him. Imagine that you are with a group of your closest friends, and one of them announces that he or she is leaving and the rest of you can't come along. Furthermore, one of you will betray that person and another will deny ever knowing him or her. How would you react?

I know that I would be confused, hurt, angry, and afraid. I would have a lot of questions and wonder why my friend was abandoning me. If that friend went on to say, in effect, "but don't be upset, there's nothing to fear, someone else will replace me," I would probably laugh bitterly and make a sarcastic remark.

Jesus' words are all the more remarkable to us because we know the rest of the story. He is about to be arrested, beaten, mocked, and killed, yet here he is wanting to comfort and reassure his friends, even though he knows they will betray, deny, and abandon him. He is preparing them for what is to come by giving them a peace that only he can give and telling them not to let their hearts be troubled or afraid.

If only it were that easy! Wouldn't it be nice if we could simply choose not to let our hearts be troubled or afraid ever again? The reality is that when we face stressful situations, no matter how hard we try to stay calm and keep from being fearful, there are times that our hearts are greatly troubled and we cannot help but be afraid.

The same was true for Jesus' disciples, despite his words. After his death, they were so afraid that they were meeting behind locked doors! However, they did not let their fears keep them from proclaiming the good news about Jesus.

In the same way, I think God wants each of us to face our fears and refuse to let them keep us from doing what we know is right. The peace that Jesus gives isn't the absence of doubt, fear, or conflict; it's the ability to persevere in the midst of all of those things, knowing that whatever we face, God is with us, and with God all things are possible, even resurrection from the dead.

Questions for Personal Reflection

1. Have you ever been betrayed or abandoned by a friend? If so, how did you react?

2. Is there something you feel called to do that you have avoided or put off doing because you are afraid? How can God help you overcome your fears?

3. What do you think Jesus meant when he said, "Peace I leave with you; my peace I give to you. I do not give as the world gives?" How is the peace he gives different? Have you ever experienced that peace in your life?

"O Lord, how many are my foes! Many are rising against me; many are saying to me, 'There is no help for you in God.' But you, O Lord, are a shield around me, my glory, and the one who lifts up my head. I cry aloud to the Lord, and he answers me from his holy hill. I lie down and sleep; I wake again, for the Lord sustains me."

Psalm 3:1-5

I have a keychain with a photo of a sleeping cat and the words, "RELAX! It's all in God's hands," followed by the last verse quoted above. I have another one with the serenity prayer on one side and a drawing of a director's chair with God's name on it and the words, "RELAX, God is in charge." Whenever I drive my car, or lock or unlock my front door, I can't help but see those words. That's a good thing, because I need all the reminders I can get to relax, stop worrying, and trust God to see me through whatever is currently stressing me out!

David, the presumed writer of this Psalm (and many others), had more stress in his life than most people do. Psalm 3 is said to have been written when David was in danger of being killed by his son Absalom. Yes, his own son was trying to kill him; Absalom was eager to seize power and become the next king, and had convinced the people of Israel to side with him. When David writes, "Many are rising against me," he is not exaggerating for dramatic effect; he is quite literally fleeing for his life from an army of people, led by his son, determined to kill him.

Somehow, in the midst of that, David is able to affirm that God is his shield and glory, the one who lifts up his head and answers him when he cries aloud. He is even able to say, "I lie down and sleep; I wake again, for the Lord sustains me."

I love the description of God as "the one who lifts up my head." Do you ever have days when you are so deep in despair or so worried about something that you really don't even want to lift your head off of the pillow, get up, and face another day? I know I do. There are times when I would much rather burrow under the covers and go back to sleep, because it seems like that's the only way I can escape some unpleasant realities and avoid dealing with life's challenges. At other times, I feel so guilty about what I have said or done (or what I have NOT done that I think I should have), or so hurt by what someone else has said or done to me, that I want to hang my head in shame or sorrow. The only reason I make it through those days is because God sustains me.

God sustains each of us every single day of our lives. We may not always be aware of God's presence, or recognize the ways in which God answers our cries, but there is indeed help for us in God.

Questions for Personal Reflection

1. How has God sustained you in the past? How is God present in your life today?

2. Who are the foes rising against you? How does God shield you and help you lift up your head as you interact with those people?

"Let no evil talk come out of your mouths, but only what is useful for building up, as there is need, so that your words may give grace to those who hear. And do not grieve the Holy Spirit of God, with which you were marked with a seal for the day of redemption. Put away from you all bitterness and wrath and anger and wrangling and slander, together with all malice, and be kind to one another, tenderhearted, forgiving one another, as God in Christ has forgiven you. Therefore be imitators of God, as beloved children, and live in love, as Christ loved us and gave himself up for us, a fragrant offering and sacrifice to God."

Ephesians 4:29-5:2

There are times when my words do give grace to those who hear, and I rejoice that God has used me to bring comfort and hope to others. As my husband knows all too well, however, there are also times when I say things in anger and am far from being kind, tenderhearted, and forgiving! I'm sure the same is true for you.

As we look at this passage, it's important to note that even Jesus got angry at times and spoke some harsh words. He called the scribes and Pharisees a brood of vipers, evil, hypocrites, and blind guides. He told the money changers in the temple that they had made it a den of robbers, overturned their tables, and drove them out. He referred to an entire generation of people as evil and adulterous. On one occasion, he even said to Peter, "Get behind me, Satan!"

There are times when anger is an appropriate response. What we do with our anger makes all the difference, and we can learn a lot from how Jesus handled his anger. He expressed it directly to the people with whom he was angry, rather than badmouthing them behind their backs and pretending everything was fine when he saw them in person. He did not beat up or kill anyone. He did not hold grudges or plot revenge against those who wronged him.

As followers of Jesus, we are called to model our lives after his. When we put away bitterness and wrath and anger and wrangling and slander, and are kind to one another, tenderhearted, and forgiving, we are obedient to God, set a good example, and create a better community and ultimately a better world. We also live happier, healthier lives; when we are able to let go of our anger, stop dwelling on past wrongs or thinking about how we can get even, and move on with our lives we benefit at least as much as the person against whom we harbored resentment does.

The key is to live in love. When we love the way that Christ loves us, we listen respectfully to others, find common ground and continue to work together even when we disagree on a particular issue, treat others the way we would want to be treated even when they treat us badly, and seek ways to build up individuals and the community as a whole.

Questions for Personal Reflection

1. When have you spoken words that build people up? What was the response to your words, and how did you feel?

2. When have you let evil talk come out of your mouth? What was the response, and how did you feel?

3. How does God help you put away bitterness, slander, and malice, and be kind, tenderhearted, and forgiving?

"Be gracious to me, O Lord, for I am languishing; O Lord, heal me, for my bones are shaking with terror. My soul also is struck with terror, while you, O Lord – how long? Turn, O Lord, save my life; deliver me for the sake of your steadfast love."

Psalm 6:2-4

"Are we there yet?" "How much longer?" My parents got asked those questions frequently when I was growing up, because I'm the oldest of six children and every summer my family would drive to Florida to vacation at the beach. The drive took anywhere from 4 ½ to 6 hours, depending on how many times we had to stop along the way, and we were always impatient to get there.

David, the presumed writer of this Psalm, wants to know how much longer he'll have to wait for God to intervene and save his life. These days it seems like there are a lot of people wondering when things will start to get better in their lives. Some of us are wondering how long it will take to find work, and how we'll pay our bills in the meantime. Others are wondering how much longer a loved one will suffer before dying from a terminal illness. Still others wonder how they'll cope after a natural disaster has devastated their community. The list could go on and on; almost everyone faces some situation that causes them to question how much longer they'll have to endure it and why God doesn't seem to be doing anything to help them.

I have yet to hear a fully satisfactory answer to the question of why bad things happen to good people. There are two general explanations that I've heard over the years: one is that God causes the bad things, either to punish people for their sins or because it is part of some cosmic master plan that we humans can't understand since we don't know everything that God knows; the other is that bad things just happen, either as the natural consequences of human sinfulness, or as random chance events, and God grieves with us and works to bring good out of those tragic situations.

Maybe when we see God face to face, we'll finally get a full explanation, but I'm not sure it really matters. Whatever their cause, when bad things happen to us, we just want our suffering to end. In most cases, though, we are not able to know in advance how long it will take before things get better; we can only trust that God will deliver us somehow. Often that deliverance comes in a way that we did not expect and may not even want, and it may require us to make some difficult choices and go in a different direction than we had planned. The one constant in our lives is God's steadfast love, and sometimes all we can do is cling to that when everything else is crumbling around us, and trust that God will bring new life out of the ruins.

Questions for Personal Reflection

1. What strikes your soul with terror? Do you feel God's presence with you as you face that terror?

2. From what have you asked God to deliver you? How has God responded?

3. How do you explain why bad things happen to good people? What is God's role in human suffering?

"And we urge you, beloved, to admonish the idlers, encourage the faint hearted, help the weak, be patient with all of them. See that none of you repays evil for evil, but always seek to do good to one another and to all. Rejoice always, pray without ceasing, give thanks in all circumstances; for this is the will of God in Christ Jesus for you."

1 Thessalonians 5:14-18

If all of us were able to take these words to heart and consistently live by them, our churches, communities, countries, and the world in general would be much better off. So would each of us as individuals. Do you remember when neighbors knew each other well, watched out for each other's children, and checked on elderly neighbors who lived alone? Perhaps you're fortunate enough to live in a community where that is still the norm, but many of us don't even know all of our neighbors' names; at most we say hello to them in passing, but we probably would not feel comfortable asking them for help.

These words were written to a church family, and in an ideal world church members would know each other well enough to know what is going on in each other's lives, sense when something is wrong, and offer admonishment, encouragement, and help as needed. In my experience, though, that is not always the case. Sometimes that is because church members who need help are embarrassed to ask for it and prefer to hide their pain and pretend everything is fine; sometimes it's because members are simply too busy coping with their own family's problems, or with the normal demands of everyday life, to have the time or energy to reach out and help someone else.

I have, however, seen some remarkable examples of church members coming together to support each other during tough times, especially when a loved one has died. I have also seen members doing things like collecting food for the local food pantry to help people they've never met. My own family was helped by people from a congregation at which I had only worshipped once or twice while home from college; when my mom was hospitalized, after I had gone back to school, members of that church brought food to my dad and my younger siblings, even though the rest of my family had never worshipped there.

For me, while it can certainly be challenging to "always seek to do good to one another and to all," it is even more challenging to "rejoice always, pray without ceasing, give thanks in all circumstances." That's another reason why community is so important. The "you" in verse 14 is plural, and throughout the Bible that is usually the case. The word "saint" only appears once in the entire Bible, while "saints" appears numerous times; the idea that one could be an individual follower of Christ without belonging to a community of believers was simply unimaginable back then.

Some people may be content to get their support from family and friends, or some other community to which they belong, and worship God on their own, but I can't imagine not belonging to a community of faith that gathers together to worship at least once each week. When I don't feel much like rejoicing or giving thanks for my present circumstances, participating in the songs, liturgy, and prayers of the church, hearing the sermon, receiving Holy Communion, and interacting with people before and after worship gives me reason to rejoice and give thanks, calms my fears, and gives me the strength and encouragement I need to make it through the rest of the week.

Questions for Personal Reflection

1. How do you admonish the idlers, encourage the faint hearted, and help the weak? In what ways do you seek to do good to all?

2. How do others admonish, encourage, or otherwise help you? Are you more likely to turn to family, friends, or the church when you need help?

3. Is it really possible to rejoice always, pray without ceasing, and give thanks in all circumstances? How do you do that during tough times when you're not feeling happy or grateful?

"Do not let loyalty and faithfulness forsake you; bind them around your neck, write them on the tablet of your heart. So you will find favor and good repute in the sight of God and of people. Trust in the Lord with all your heart, and do not rely on your own insight. In all your ways acknowledge him, and he will direct your paths."

Proverbs 3:3-6

"Bind them around your neck, write them on the tablet of your heart." How's that for evocative imagery? Scripture is full of poetic language, and this phrase is one of my favorites. Obviously, the point is to stress the importance of loyalty and faithfulness, and this writer has found a memorable way to do that.

We know what it means to be loyal to a friend, or faithful to a spouse, but what does it mean to "not let loyalty and faithfulness forsake you?" I think it entails making loyalty and faithfulness an integral part of who we are, qualities that are evident in all of our interactions. It comes down to keeping our word, honoring our commitments, and living lives that are true to our beliefs. When we are able to do that, we do indeed find favor and good repute in God's eyes and the eyes of people.

The next piece of advice in these verses is to trust God with all your heart, and not rely on your own insight. Have you ever felt that God was challenging you to do something, perhaps even something you truly wanted to do, but you didn't do it because you were convinced that it was too risky, or too expensive, or not feasible for some other reason? I have, and when I followed my head instead of my heart I was miserable. When I trusted God and did what I felt led to do, even though it seemed crazy (like when my husband and I resigned as pastors, sold our house in Pennsylvania, and moved to Maui without having jobs or a place to live lined up in advance), things always worked out somehow and I never regretted the choice. God truly does direct our paths; the only question is whether or not we are willing to trust God and follow those paths without fully knowing where they will lead.

Questions for Personal Reflection

1. Do you consider yourself loyal and faithful? Do you think others would describe you that way?

2. Have you ever had to choose between trusting God and relying on your own insight? If so, what choice did you make and what were the results?

3. How do you acknowledge God in your daily life? How does God direct your paths?

"Finally, beloved, whatever is true, whatever is honorable, whatever is just, whatever is pure, whatever is pleasing, whatever is commendable, if there is any excellence and if there is anything worthy of praise, think about these things. Keep on doing the things that you have learned and received and heard and seen in me, and the God of peace will be with you."

Philippians 4:8-9

I must confess that I tend to see the glass as half empty, not half full. My husband jokes that instead of looking for the silver lining, I look for the gray lining in a cloud full of silver, and he's right; I do tend to be a pessimist. I am making a genuine effort to change that, and focus on the positive, but lately it seems more and more challenging to find things worthy of praise.

When I do look for them, though, I discover that there are, in fact, still plenty of good things happening, both in my life and in the wider world. If you doubt that, do a Google search for "good news stories" and check out a few of the sites. You'll find a whole host of stories about individuals and organizations doing wonderful things. I checked while writing this and found an article about a non-profit organization helping military families in need, another about advances in cancer research, and one about a virtual reality computer game that helps burn patients take their minds off their pain. If you don't have internet access, there are plenty of inspiring books available, too; collections of stories like the popular *Chicken Soup for the Soul* series are a good place to start.

There is a Cherokee legend about a boy being taught how to handle anger by his grandfather. I've heard several different versions of it, but the heart of the story is that the grandfather says it is as if two wolves are at war inside him; one that is loving, kind, full of faith and hope, and always sees the best in people, and another that is angry, jealous, greedy, arrogant, and evil. The boy anxiously asks which wolf will win the fight, and the grandfather replies, "the one that you feed."

I think the same is true in our minds. We can choose to look at the world and see all that is wrong; focus on the greed and corruption, rapes, murders and other criminal activity, and widespread poverty and hunger, addiction and unemployment. We can also choose to focus our attention on the people who have overcome remarkable odds to make great contributions to society, the everyday heroes who risk their own lives to save others, those who give generously of their time and money to help people they may never meet, and the countless other examples of excellence worthy of praise. Clearly, God wants us to choose the latter.

Questions for Personal Reflection

1. Do you consider yourself more of an optimist or a pessimist?

2. Which of the two wolves mentioned in the story are you currently feeding?

3. How can God help you think about whatever is true, honorable, just, pure, pleasing, and commendable? Where do you currently see things worthy of praise?

"I will stand at my watchpost, and station myself on the rampart; I will keep watch to see what he will say to me, and what he will answer concerning my complaint. Then the Lord answered me and said: Write the vision; make it plain on tablets, so that a runner may read it. For there is still a vision for the appointed time; it speaks of the end, and does not lie. If it seems to tarry, wait for it; it will surely come, it will not delay. Look at the proud! Their spirit is not right in them, but the righteous live by their faith."

Habakkuk 2:1-4

This is another instance in the Bible where someone who is fed up with the violence, wrongdoing, and injustice he sees all around him asks God how long his cries for help will go unheard. The complaint referenced in the first verse is lengthy (for context, read Habakkuk 1:1 – 17), but it boils down to a demand that God answer the question, "Why do you look on the treacherous, and are silent when the wicked swallow those more righteous than they?"

Sound familiar? I think a lot of people are wondering the same thing today. Too often, it seems that profits are valued above people, wealth and power are concentrated in the hands of a select few who use their influence to ensure that it stays that way, and arrogant government leaders cater to the wishes of that elite group instead of the needs of the overwhelming majority of people.

So how does God respond to Habakkuk's complaint? God makes it clear that God still has a vision, and at the right time it will become a reality. Furthermore, even though the greedy and arrogant may be prospering now, at some point they will reap what they have sown. The verses following the ones quoted here are directed at those "who heap up what is not your own," and pose provocative questions like, "Will not your own creditors suddenly rise, and those who make you tremble wake up?" and state unequivocally, "Because you have plundered many nations, all that survive of the peoples shall plunder you." (Habakkuk 2:6-8)

Whatever the future holds, we know who holds the future, and that enables us to live by faith as we wait for God's vision to appear.

Questions for Personal Reflection

1. Have you ever complained to God? How did God respond?

2. What is your vision for the future? How do you think it compares to God's vision?

3. What does it mean to live by your faith? How do you do that?

"And you, child, shall be called the prophet of the most high, for you will go before the Lord to prepare his ways, to give knowledge of salvation to his people by the forgiveness of their sins. By the tender mercy of our God, the dawn from on high will break upon us, to give light to those who sit in darkness and the shadow of death, to guide our feet into the way of peace."

Luke 1:76-79

Zechariah spoke these words about his son John when John was less than two weeks old. The angel Gabriel, the same angel who visited Mary to announce that she would conceive and bear a son named Jesus, had visited Zechariah to announce that Zechariah's wife Elizabeth would bear a son, who was to be named John, and that John would "be great in the sight of the Lord" and "make ready a people prepared for the Lord." (Zechariah 1:15, 17) Because Zechariah did not believe this at first, he was unable to speak from that moment until eight days after John's birth, when Zechariah praised God.

Zechariah had good reason to doubt; their marriage had been childless and Elizabeth was now too old to have a child without divine intervention. Once he saw that the seemingly impossible had actually happened, though, Zechariah had no trouble believing the rest of the angel's speech about what John would do, and John the Baptist, as he is usually called because he baptized so many people, did in fact preach repentance for the forgiveness of sins.

Notice that John gives knowledge of salvation to people by the forgiveness of their sins. Salvation doesn't come from living a perfect, sin-free life; it comes from acknowledging one's sins, repenting (which means changing one's ways, not just saying "I'm sorry"), and then receiving God's forgiveness. We don't earn that forgiveness; it is a gift given to us.

It is by God's mercy, not our own actions, that the dawn from on high breaks upon us and brings light to those who sit in darkness and the shadow of death. This is not just a future hope for a better life in heaven; God's forgiveness transforms our present-day lives and makes dramatic reconciliations and new beginnings possible here and now.

At the same time, I'm always amazed when I talk with lifelong Christians who know that death is near, or are contemplating what life after death will be like for some other reason, perhaps after a friend's funeral, and they say, "Well, I hope I'll make it to heaven. I've tried to live a good life." The reality is that none of us will go to heaven because we've lived a good life! No matter how good we are, we aren't good enough; if we could do it on our own, why would we need a Savior? We don't have to hope we've done enough to earn a place in heaven; Christ has already gone to prepare a place for us, and we have a guaranteed reservation! Once we realize that, we are free to serve others out of a genuine desire for God to use us to spread the news of God's love and forgiveness, and as a grateful response for all that God has done for us, instead of to avoid punishment or earn brownie points with God.

Questions for Personal Reflection

1. Do you consider yourself a prophet? In what way do you prepare the way of the Lord, or give people knowledge of salvation?

2. How has God brought light to you during dark times in your life? How have you shared that light with others?

3. Do you believe you'll go to heaven? Why or why not?

"Rise up, O Lord; O God, lift up your hand; do not forget the oppressed. Why do the wicked renounce God, and say in their hearts, 'You will not call us to account'? But you do see! Indeed you note trouble and grief, that you may take it into your hands; the helpless commit themselves to you; you have been the helper of the orphan."

Psalm 10:12-14

Do you know the song, "He's Got the Whole World in His Hands"? It's a children's song that I remember singing in Sunday School and Vacation Bible School. Each verse highlights a different group of people (the two that come to mind immediately are "little bitty babies" and "everybody here") held in God's hands, and the stanzas always end with the phrase, "He's got the whole world in his hands."

I thought of that song as soon as I saw the words "Indeed you note trouble and grief, that you may take it into your hands" in today's reading. I believe that our trouble and grief is truly in God's hands; the question is what does God do with it? Sometimes, God intervenes in dramatic and totally unexpected ways; my husband and I recently experienced this when people called us and volunteered to help us out financially just when it looked like we would not be able to pay our health insurance premium and would lose our coverage. I know of someone else who had a cancer discovered in time to operate and save his life only because he has a friend who is a radiologist, and that friend wanted to demonstrate what he does for a living by screening him. He had no symptoms and doctors were amazed the cancer was detected so early and said otherwise he would have been dead in a few months!

Most of the time, though, God doesn't keep us from experiencing trouble and grief; instead, God goes through it with us and helps us cope. I have other friends who have died of cancer, often after a great deal of suffering, and plenty of people have lost their health insurance, their homes, and even their lives because they didn't have enough money to pay for basic necessities. God's help for the helpless does not mean that nothing bad will ever happen; Jesus and his disciples experienced plenty of trouble and grief in their lives.

God's help takes many forms: a card, phone call, or visit from a friend; caring doctors, nurses, clergy, counselors, and other professionals; the words of a song, sermon, or prayer you hear at just the right time; and so many other possibilities that I couldn't begin to list them all. It is not just our trouble and grief that is in God's hands, *we* are in God's hands, and God lovingly carries us through good times and bad.

Questions for Personal Reflection

1. Have you ever felt helpless? What were the circumstances?

2. How has God seen your trouble and grief, and helped you?

3. What does it mean to commit yourself to God? How does making that commitment change your life, and how do you honor that commitment in your daily life?

"After our baptism, an even greater baptism – if I may make so bold as to put it that way – is the baptism provided by our tears. Our first baptism cleansed all our former sins….The baptism of our tears cleanses us anew by the gift of compassion God gives to the human race."

St. John Klimakos[1]

Have you ever experienced the death of someone close to you, like a spouse, parent, or child? If so, you know how devastating that loss is, and I'm sure you have shed many tears over the years. Now think about the people who comforted you as you grieved. Chances are, those who were most helpful to you were the ones who had experienced a similar loss in their own lives.

If you haven't experienced the death of a loved one, think of another situation in your life that was deeply upsetting and brought you to tears, like finding out your partner cheated on you, or facing your own or a loved one's addiction, or losing your job or your home. Who helped you get through that? My guess is that it was someone who had survived something similar.

Of course, that is not to say that no one can give you support and encouragement unless they have experienced the same thing; it's just that those who have are able to empathize with your feelings and understand your needs in a way that those who have not cannot. That is one of the reasons that 12-step groups are so effective; someone who has been where you are is able to share their story and prove that it really is possible to change your life.

Naturally, no one wants to experience the death of a loved one, losing their job or home, being betrayed by a partner, or dealing with an addiction. If we could somehow look at a list of possible life events and choose the ones we'd like to experience, we would pick the joyous ones. However, it is usually the most difficult times in our lives that lead to the greatest growth, and spur us on to accomplish things we never would have even attempted otherwise.

If nothing else, we become more compassionate and aware of our human limitations. There is a kind of cleansing we experience when our tears force us to acknowledge how sad and vulnerable we are, and to reach out to others for help. Our own experience of suffering also makes us more likely to be able to offer meaningful words of comfort and hope when someone else needs our help.

Questions for Personal Reflection

1. When was the last time you cried? Did your tears cleanse you?

2. Would you describe compassion as a gift God gives to the human race? Why or why not?

3. How have your own times of sorrow changed how you respond to others who are grieving, especially those going through something similar to what you experienced?

"If your mind can pray without distraction, your heart will soon be softened. And, as it says in scripture: 'God will never scorn a heart that is humbled and distressed.'"

Mark the Ascetic

I would love to be able to pray without distraction. Every now and then, when I stick with it long enough, I do manage to do that, but those occasions are few and far between. Most of the time, my mind is racing in all kinds of different directions. Instead of concentrating on talking with God, it is reviewing my to-do list for the day, compiling a grocery list, reminding me I need to call my sister to wish her happy birthday, and so on.

I've talked with enough people over the years to know that this problem is not unique to me. We are so used to doing several things at once – reading emails while talking on the phone, with the TV or music on in the background, for instance – that it has become increasingly difficult for us to quiet our minds and focus intently and exclusively on praying. It's quicker and easier to recite a prayer we have memorized than it is to have an in-depth conversation with God, sharing all that is on our minds and in our hearts and listening for God's response.

The rewards of having that in-depth conversation make it well worth the effort, though. When I have been able to do it, my heart has indeed been softened. I have become calmer, more patient with others, less irritable, more willing to forgive, and better able to recognize and give thanks for all of the ways in which God has blessed me, even during the most difficult times of my life.

You've probably heard the saying, "Prayer changes things." I would argue that prayer changes *us*, so that we become empowered to change things for the better when possible, and find the lessons to be learned and the opportunities for personal growth in unpleasant circumstances that we cannot change.

Questions for Personal Reflection

1. What distracts you when you pray? How do you deal with the distraction?

2. How has prayer changed you?

"If you are tired and worn out by your labors for your Lord, place your head upon his knee and rest awhile. Recline upon his breast, breathe in the fragrant spirit of life, and allow life to permeate your being. Rest upon him, for he is a table of refreshment that will serve you the food of the Divine Father."

John of Dalyutha[3]

Just reading these words at the end of a stressful day soothes me. It is easy to visualize myself with my head on Jesus' knee, or leaning against him and resting on his breast. He radiates such calm, and is so clearly at peace that I can't help but feel peaceful when I am near him.

Take a moment to literally picture yourself with your head on Jesus' knee, or reclining on his breast. What are you wearing? What is the expression on your face, and on Jesus' face? Does Jesus speak to you? Do you say anything to Jesus? Where are you, and what do you see, hear, and smell? Stay in the scene as long as possible, and pay attention to every detail. Savor the experience, and thank God for it.

The wonderful truth is that each and every one of us is actually in Jesus' presence every moment of our lives. It's easy to forget that when we are busy running errands, taking care of children, answering emails, and doing all of the other tasks of life. However, the fact that we sometimes fail to recognize that Jesus is with us doesn't change the reality that he is always near, eager to pull us close and encouraging us to rest upon him.

When we allow ourselves to do that, we are refreshed and reminded that we are loved. We are able to pause and "breathe in the fragrant spirit of life." Most of all, we are comforted and reassured by the knowledge that no matter what we may be facing, we do not face it alone.

Questions for Personal Reflection

1. What was it like for you to picture yourself with your head on Jesus' knee or reclining on his breast? How did you feel before, during, and after the experience?

2. What does it mean to you to "breathe in the fragrant spirit of life, and allow life to permeate your being"? How do you do that?

3. What do you think the "food of the Divine Father" is? How is Jesus the "table of refreshment" that serves it to you?

"As God's chosen ones, holy and beloved, clothe yourselves with compassion, kindness, humility, meekness, and patience. Bear with one another and, if anyone has a complaint against another, forgive each other; just as the Lord has forgiven you, so you also must forgive. Above all, clothe yourselves with love, which binds everything together in perfect harmony. And let the peace of Christ rule in your hearts, to which indeed you were called in the one body. And be thankful."

Colossians 3:12-15

One thing I dreaded as a child was when we played some kind of sport during gym class at school. The teacher would name two team captains, and they would take turns choosing people to be on their teams. Suffice it to say that I was never one of the first ones chosen; it was always an ordeal for me to wait and wonder whether I would eventually be selected, or just be the person that one team was forced to take because there was no one else left.

Thankfully, we don't have to worry about whether or not God will choose us, nor do we need a history of being a star player to be considered a valuable addition to God's team. God chooses us long before we have done anything to prove ourselves. The only question is how we will respond to being chosen. Will we take our favored status for granted, or do everything we possibly can to contribute to the team's success?

This text offers us great wisdom about how to be team players; that is, to live together as the body of Christ. First, we put on our uniforms: we clothe ourselves with compassion, kindness, humility, meekness, and patience. To be compassionate and kind is to empathize with the suffering of people in our community and in the wider world, and find ways to do ministry with them. To be humble is to acknowledge that none of us has all the answers, to seek consensus whenever possible, and to seek to know and do God's will above all else, recognizing that God's will may be different from ours. To be meek is to be gentle and willing to work together to get things done without worrying about who gets the credit. Last but not least, to be patient is to be willing to wait, and do things God's way and on God's timetable.

Next we are advised to bear with one another, and forgive each other just as the Lord has forgiven us. This is not easy. When we have been wronged, it is tempting to be angry at the person who has mistreated us, hold a grudge, and maybe even plot revenge, but when we realize how much God has forgiven us, how can we refuse to forgive others?

Most of all, we are called to clothe ourselves with love. When we love as God has first loved us, everything is connected in perfect harmony. The peace of Christ truly does rule in our hearts and we realize that we have good reason to be thankful.

Questions for Personal Reflection

1. Do you think of yourself as God's chosen one, holy and beloved? Why or why not?

2. How do you clothe yourself with compassion, kindness, humility, meekness, and patience? Which of these is easiest for you to put on, and which is most difficult?

3. What does it mean to let the peace of Christ rule in your heart? How do you do that?

"I bless the Lord who gives me counsel; in the night my heart also instructs me. I keep the Lord always before me; because he is at my right hand, I shall not be moved. Therefore my heart is glad, and my soul rejoices; my body also rests secure. For you do not give me up to Sheol, or let your faithful one see the Pit. You show me the path of life. In your presence there is fullness of joy; in your right hand are pleasures forevermore."

Psalm 16:7-11

I've often wished that I could sit across from God and get advice, or hear God speaking to me from a burning bush, or have some other clear, unmistakable message from God about what I'm supposed to do. Wouldn't it be nice if we could literally keep God always before us, available for consultation whenever we face a big decision?

The reality is that we do always have God with us; in fact, God is not only near us but also *within* us. Christian leaders are sometimes hesitant to speak that truth, because it can so easily be misinterpreted to mean that each of us *is* God, but the Bible contains multiple references to the Spirit of God dwelling in us. When we've been wondering how to handle a situation and suddenly have a moment of absolute clarity about what our next step needs to be, or we meet someone for the first time and end up having a profound experience of deep and meaningful connection when we least expect it, or when we feel absolutely compelled to call or visit someone right away and don't know why, but we do it and it turns out that they really needed our help at that moment, I believe that is God at work within us.

I also believe God sometimes speaks to us through our dreams; perhaps that is what the author of this Psalm meant when he wrote "in the night my heart also instructs me." I have had a few recurring dreams over the years, and one dream that was so powerful and wonderful that I can still recall parts of it all these years later; in both cases it has been clear that God was sending me a message. Of course, I've also had plenty of bizarre dreams that did not seem to have any relationship to reality or communicate anything other than the fact that I have a very vivid imagination!

However and whenever God communicates with us, it can be challenging to recognize God's voice. When we learn to listen for it, though, and actually heed God's counsel, we are shown the path of life.

Questions for Personal Reflection

1. How does God give you counsel? Does God most often speak to you through dreams, through other people, or in some other way?

2. How do you know when God is trying to tell you something? Is there a way that you can tell the difference between what God wants you to do, what others think you should do, and what you would like to do?

"When Mary came to where Jesus was and saw him, she knelt at his feet and said to him, 'Lord, if you had been here, my brother would not have died.' When Jesus saw her weeping, and the Jews who came with her also weeping, he was greatly disturbed in spirit and deeply moved. He said, 'Where have you laid him?' They said to him, 'Lord, come and see.' Jesus began to weep. So the Jews said, 'See how he loved him!' But some of them said, 'Could not he who opened the eyes of the blind man have kept this man from dying?'"

John 11:32-37

These verses only tell part of the story of Jesus raising Lazarus from the dead; for the full account, read John 11:1-44. Mary and Martha had sent word to Jesus that Lazarus was ill, but instead of rushing to his bedside Jesus stayed where we was for two more days, and Lazarus died. We don't know exactly what Mary was feeling, or in what tone of voice she uttered the words, "Lord, if you had been here, my brother would not have died," but every time I hear this story I picture a hurt, angry, tearful woman screaming at Jesus, saying, in effect, "You knew he was sick. Why did you wait until now to come?"

Most of us have probably had at least one experience in our lives when we, too, thought God wasn't there for us in our time of need. We were left alone to suffer, to grieve, to bear hurts that were unbearable. We waited a lot longer than the four days Mary and Martha had to wait before Jesus took away our pain. Some of us are still waiting.

When Jesus sees Mary and the Jews who came with her weeping, he is greatly disturbed in spirit and deeply moved. Then he begins to weep. Clearly, we have a God who feels our pain, who hurts when we hurt and cries with us. Jesus does more than empathize with us, though; he intervenes. While we probably won't have a loved one die and four days later be brought back to live with us on earth, with God's help new life will come out of the most difficult and heartbreaking times in our lives, often in dramatic and unexpected ways.

It is hard to trust Christ's promise of new life. Just as Martha questioned the wisdom of rolling away the stone at the entrance to Lazarus' tomb, we hesitate to roll away the stones in our own lives that keep us trapped. Whatever our own stones may be, when we do risk rolling them away we find that God is there for us after all, often in ways we never could have imagined.

We have a God who not only grieves with us but also acts to save us. And even though that process usually takes longer and hurts more than we'd like, out of it comes the new life we've been promised.

Questions for Personal Reflection

1. How do you explain Jesus' decision not to go immediately to be with Lazarus, or to prevent his death?

2. Have you ever prayed for God to heal a loved one who was ill and later died? How did that affect your faith?

3. What are the stones in your life now that need to be removed so that you are able to experience new life?

"When it was evening on that day, the first day of the week, and the doors of the house where the disciples had met were locked for fear of the Jews, Jesus came and stood among them and said, 'Peace be with you.' After he said this, he showed them his hands and his side. Then the disciples rejoiced when they saw the Lord. Jesus said to them again, 'Peace be with you. As the Father has sent me, so I send you.'"

John 20:19-21

"Peace be with you." Those were Jesus' first words to his disciples when he appeared to them after his resurrection. Imagine. Their world had just been turned upside-down. Their master, their teacher, their friend, had been killed. The man they expected to deliver them from the hands of their Roman oppressors had himself been handed over to be crucified, and they had been powerless to stop it. Worse yet, some of the disciples themselves were the very ones who betrayed Jesus, and abandoned him in his hour of need. In addition to their sorrow, the disciples must have been filled with guilt. Surely there was also confusion, and uncertainty about what they should do next. In the midst of all of that, Jesus appears to them unexpectedly and says "peace be with you." Somehow I don't think they were feeling very peaceful! In fact, the text says that the doors were locked out of fear, and yet suddenly Jesus is there in the room with them. Once they realized who he was, they rejoiced, but they must have been terrified at first.

He could have waited until they felt some sense of security and normalcy before saying "Peace be with you." Instead, he appeared during their most difficult days, as they were coping with conflicting emotions and wondering how they could go on when all of their dreams had been shattered. I believe he does the same with us.

He breaks into our lives, even when we try to shut him out, and keeps appearing until we believe. The disciples did not believe the women at the tomb when they claimed to have seen the risen Lord, so Jesus appeared to the disciples. Thomas wasn't there that night, and he refused to believe the other disciples, so Jesus appeared to him. While we may not be able to see the mark of the nails in His hands, or put our hands in His side, we are able to see Jesus in the midst of our own troubled times. Some of us literally see a vision of Jesus, some experience events that can't possibly be just coincidences, and some know Christ is with us through the actions of caring family, friends, and even strangers. Christ appears in all kinds of different ways, and we don't always recognize him at first, but he is with us.

Christ says more than just "Peace be with you," though. He also says, "As the Father has sent me, so I send you." Christ calls us to share the peace that we have received, so that others may also discover that there is hope, no matter how bad things get. Many people will refuse to believe that Christ has risen until they see for themselves. Our task is to make Christ's presence visible to all the doubting, sorrowing people out there, by sharing the peace that only He can give. May the Holy Spirit empower each of us to overcome the fear that keeps us behind locked doors, and guide us in our efforts to share the love of Christ with everyone we encounter.

Questions for Personal Reflection

1. How and when does Jesus appear to you? Is it easier for you to recognize his presence when things are going well or when times are tough?

2. How do you share Christ's love and peace with others?

"If I had everything that I could desire, and my finger ached, I should not have everything, for I should have a pain in my finger, and so long as that remained, I should not enjoy full comfort. Bread is comfortable for men, when they are hungry; but when they are thirsty, they find no more comfort in bread than in a stone. So it is with clothes, they are welcome to men, when they are cold; but when they are too hot, clothes give them no comfort. And so it is with all the creatures. The comfort which they promise is only on the surface, like froth, and it always carries with it a want. But God's comfort is clear and has nothing wanting: it is full and complete, and God is constrained to give it thee, for He cannot cease till He have given thee Himself."

Meister Eckhart

Eckhart was a thirteenth century German mystic and priest. Obviously, the world in which he lived was very different from our world today. However, I think these words of his are very applicable to life now.

Have you ever had the experience of getting something you really wanted, enjoying it immensely for a few days, or weeks, or months, and then largely forgetting about it as your thoughts turned to obtaining something else? Perhaps the best example of this is kids opening gifts at Christmas. They can't wait, and are so excited when they first see the toy for which they have been longing. They play with that toy all day, show it off to their friends, and absolutely adore it, but a few months later it sits abandoned next to other toys they once loved. As the next Christmas approaches, they probably don't even remember what they got the year before, because they are eagerly anticipating receiving the items on their new wish list.

As adults, we have different desires; we want things like a new car, a house, new clothes, the latest electronic gadgets, a promotion, raise, or new job, and so on. Some just want food, clean drinking water, and a safe place to live. Regardless of what we want, when we get it we aren't satisfied for long. Even if we eat the most extravagant feast imaginable and drink our fill, at some point we will be hungry and thirsty again. The new car, house, or clothes will gradually become old and need to be repaired or replaced.

God alone can give us everlasting comfort, and meet the deeper needs that no amount of money or material things will ever satisfy. God created us and continues to sustain us, whether we have more than enough or are barely surviving. God loves us unconditionally, understands us completely, and continually invites us into a closer relationship. God is always there for us, every day of our lives, through all of our trials and tribulations. God satisfies us in a way that nothing and no one else ever could.

Questions for Personal Reflection

1. What do you currently desire most? How would having it change your life?

2. Do you have items you no longer want or need? Is there a homeless shelter or other non-profit organization that could use those items?

3. How does God comfort you? What needs do you have that only God can fully satisfy?

"Jerusalem, Jerusalem, the city that kills the prophets and stones those who are sent to it! How often have I desired to gather your children together as a hen gathers her brood under her wings, and you were not willing!"

Luke 13:34

Have you ever seen a mother hen with her chicks? Baby chicks are adorable, and it is touching to watch their mother keeping them close by her side, clucking to summon them back when they wander too far away, and sheltering them protectively under her wing. Her selfless devotion to them actually begins even before they hatch. Did you know that hens spend all day and night sitting on their eggs, regularly turning them, and only leave the nest once a day, for no longer than an hour, to get food and water? Did you know that a mother hen will literally give her life for her chicks?

It is not surprising, then, that as he weeps over Jerusalem, Jesus compares himself to a mother hen longing to gather her brood under her wings. He knows that his brood is unwilling to accept that shelter, however, and will insist on going its own way. He also knows how much they will suffer, and is deeply saddened by their decision.

It is easy to read this and wonder how the people of Jerusalem could be so foolish. Jesus was right there, calling to them, but instead of eagerly flocking to him, they turned against him. Why would they do that?

It is not so easy to acknowledge that we do the same thing. In a variety of ways, and for a variety of reasons, each of us ignores God's call and heads off in another direction instead. Sometimes, we don't hear God at all, because we have stopped listening for God's voice. We are so busy juggling the demands of work or school and family and church and other activities, and listening to the voices of all of the other people in our lives, that we don't take the time to be still and listen to what God is saying to us. We always have someplace else we need to go or something else we need to do.

We may also hear God's voice, but choose to tune it out. Have you ever known someone who had "selective hearing"? For instance, many spouses and children who otherwise hear perfectly fine mysteriously become deaf when they are asked to take out the garbage, wash the dishes, clean their room, or do their homework. In the same way, when God calls us to do something we'd rather not, we may pretend not to hear.

The good news is that whenever we acknowledge our need for God and become willing to be welcomed back into the fold, we are lovingly gathered back under God's wings, no matter how many times we stray. This is one way in which the comparison to a mother hen's love for her chicks falls short; her devotion only lasts for about six weeks or so, then the mother hen decides she has had enough and it is time for the chicks to survive on their own, without any help from her.

We are fortunate that God in Christ is not like that. Jesus' devotion to us never ends. He doesn't get tired of us, abandon us, and force us to fend for ourselves. He stays with us throughout our lives, and even after we die.

Questions for Personal Reflection

1. What is God's message of motherly concern to you right now?

2. Are you more likely to run to God for comfort and shelter in difficult times, or turn away from God?

3. Are you willing to be gathered together with others by Jesus, or do you see your faith as a personal and private one-on-one relationship with God?

"Do not be ashamed, then, of the testimony about our Lord or of me his prisoner, but join with me in suffering for the gospel, relying on the power of God, who saved us and called us with a holy calling, not according to our works but according to his own purpose and grace. This grace was given to us in Christ Jesus before the ages began, but it has now been revealed through the appearing of our Savior Christ Jesus, who abolished death and brought life and immortality to light through the gospel."

2 Timothy 1:8-10

Most of us will not be imprisoned or put to death because of the gospel. Perhaps we won't get certain jobs if we refuse to work on Sunday mornings (I have personally experienced this more than once), and maybe our beliefs will be mocked, but we are not likely to suffer in the same way that many of Jesus' early followers did. Nevertheless, I believe these verses have much to say to us.

First, we are told to rely on the power of God. Too often we rely solely on our own efforts, and blame ourselves when we don't get the results we had hoped for when we share our faith, invite someone to church, or start a new ministry. It's important to remember that the actions we take now may not yield results until years later, and sometimes we never know how much something we said or did meant to someone, or how it ultimately helped lead them to faith. Our role is to plant the seed, and trust God to do the rest.

Next, we are reminded that God saves us and calls us with a holy calling. Some of us are used to thinking of a holy calling as something unique to priests or other religious leaders, but nothing could be further from the truth. The reality is that God calls each and every believer to preach the gospel. Some of us use the written or spoken word to do so; others use actions like feeding the hungry, visiting those in prison, advocating for changes to unjust laws or labor practices, and raising money to provide mosquito nets or life-saving vaccines, medications, safe drinking water, or other necessities. Even if all we do is treat every person we encounter with respect, and recognize that they are God's beloved children even if they are rude, cut us off in traffic, or otherwise annoy us, we are proclaiming the gospel by the way we live our lives.

Finally, lest we despair over our failure to consistently live out our calling to faithfully proclaim the gospel in word and deed, and fear that our shortcomings will cause God to reject us, these verses also make it clear that we are saved "not according to our works but according to his own purpose and grace." Not only was this grace given to us before we were born, and thus clearly before we could possibly do anything to make ourselves worthy of being saved, it was given to us "before the ages began." We were part of God's plan from the very beginning, and we continue to be part of a larger plan that is beyond anything we can imagine.

Questions for Personal Reflection

1. Do you think of yourself as one who has a holy calling? If so, what is it and how do you live it out?

2. Are there times when you are ashamed of the testimony of our Lord, or afraid to share the gospel? If so, how can you overcome your fear and embarrassment and proclaim your faith outside of church settings?

3. Do you believe you are saved according to God's grace and not because of your works? Why or why not?

"Then turning toward the woman, he (Jesus) said to Simon, 'Do you see this woman? I entered your house; you gave me no water for my feet, but she has bathed my feet with her tears and dried them with her hair. You gave me no kiss, but from the time I came in she has not stopped kissing my feet. You did not anoint my head with oil, but she has anointed my feet with ointment. Therefore, I tell you, her sins, which were many, have been forgiven; hence she has shown great love. But the one to whom little is forgiven, loves little...And he said to the woman, 'Your faith has saved you; go in peace.'"

Luke 7:44-47, 50

Clearly, the woman who stands at Jesus' feet, weeping, and proceeds to bathe his feet with her tears, dry them with her hair, kiss them and anoint them with oil is courageous. She knows that she is a sinner, yet she bravely shows up uninvited at Simon the Pharisee's house because she has learned that Jesus is having dinner there. She dares to not only approach Jesus, but to use her tears to wash his feet and her hair to dry them. Then she literally kisses his feet! Out of gratitude for all that Jesus has done for her, she is willing to devote herself to him completely.

It's a touching story, and it would be easy to emphasize the fact that all of us are sinners but Jesus forgives us and wants us to love others the way that he loves us, and leave it at that. Yes, Jesus accepts the woman as she is, but he also tells her, "Your faith has saved you; go in peace." This statement, combined with the fact that Jesus tells Simon that her sins have been forgiven and therefore she has shown great love, suggests that her life changed dramatically; she did not simply express her devotion to Jesus one day and go back to living the same sinful live the next day.

It is not enough for us to express our thanksgiving for the fact that we are loved and forgiven; Jesus wants our lives to change as a result! For those of us who have been Christian for many years, and never had a dramatic experience of being "born again," it is easy to take our faith for granted. We rejoice that we are loved just as we are, and all too often we are content to leave it at that. We worship on Sundays, and perhaps pray or read our Bibles at home, but our faith is only one small part of our lives.

Like Simon, we may see ourselves as better than others that we label as sinners, and instead of reaching out to them as Jesus did, we avoid them. The truth that Jesus points out to Simon – and to us – in today's Gospel is that there is no "us" and "them." We are all sinners, and we are all God's beloved children. Jesus calls us to recognize that truth instead of running from it, because it is only when we realize the depth of our sinfulness that we can fully understand and appreciate the depth of God's love. And when we do, the only appropriate response is gratitude and complete devotion.

Questions for Personal Reflection

1. Do you have more in common with Simon, the righteous man appalled that Jesus welcomes a sinner, or with the woman who kisses Jesus' feet and anoints them with oil?

2. Visualize Jesus saying to you, "Your faith has saved you; go in peace." What are you feeling and how do you respond to him?

3. What changes do you need to make in your life to better express your gratitude and devotion to Jesus?

"Now as they went on their way, he entered a certain village, where a woman named Martha welcomed him into her home. She had a sister named Mary, who sat at the Lord's feet and listened to what he was saying. But Martha was distracted by her many tasks; so she came to him and asked, 'Lord, do you not care that my sister has left me to do all the work by myself? Tell her then to help me.' But the Lord answered her, 'Martha, Martha, you are worried and distracted by many things; there is need of only one thing. Mary has chosen the better part, which will not be taken away from her.'"

Luke 10:38-42

Surely we can sympathize with Martha in today's Gospel. She is feeling overwhelmed and frustrated that she is having to do all the work while her sister Mary sits at Jesus' feet and listens to him speak. It doesn't seem fair, and she decides to enlist Jesus' help in getting her sister to see the error of her ways, get off her butt, and help Martha get all of the household tasks done. She asks Jesus to tell Mary to help, and this seems like a reasonable request. Instead of agreeing with her and criticizing Mary's apparent laziness, though,

Jesus criticizes Martha instead! He tells her she is worried and distracted by many things, when there is need of only one thing, and that Mary has chosen the better part.

We aren't told how Martha responds. Maybe she was delighted to have permission to let the household chores go, and joined her sister at Jesus' feet to listen and learn, but somehow I doubt it. It seems more likely to me that she would have stormed out of the room, furious at his response, and perhaps said something like, "Fine. When you two are done talking you can make your own dinner and finish cleaning the house. I've got better things to do, too!"

Clearly, Luke is not suggesting that the faithful response is always to do nothing but sit at the feet of Jesus and soak up his teachings; in fact, this story is immediately preceded by the parable of the Good Samaritan. If we never act on what we learn, if we see our faith as nothing more than Jesus meeting our needs and helping us escape the stresses of our daily lives, then we will never grow in our own faith or help anyone else discover or deepen their faith.

On the other hand, if we are so busy doing our many tasks that we never take time to stop and reflect on whether what we are doing is truly most important, and never have times of rest and relaxation in which God can speak to us to renew our spirits or challenge us to reorder our priorities, our faith will also become stagnant. Jesus does not criticize Martha because of the work she is doing; he criticizes her for being worried and distracted by many things. The key is to balance sitting at the feet of Jesus and acting on what we learn there, so that we are both living out our faith and pausing to be sure that we are still hearing God's voice above all of the others competing for our attention.

Questions for Personal Reflection

1. Are you more like Martha or Mary?

2. If you sat at Jesus' feet and listened, what do you think he would say to you?

"Ask, and it will be given you; search, and you will find; knock, and the door will be opened for you. For everyone who asks receives, and everyone who searches finds, and for everyone who knocks, the door will be opened. Is there anyone among you who, if your child asks for bread, will give a stone? Or if the child asks for a fish, will give a snake? If you then, who are evil, know how to give good gifts to your children, how much more will your Father in heaven give good things to those who ask him!"

Matthew 7:7-11

These verses are sometimes interpreted to mean that we should not hesitate to ask God for anything we want, and trust that God will surely give it to us. Fortunately, God does not actually give us whatever we want. The reality is that sometimes we want things that are not good for us (or at least not as good as what God has in mind), or that might satisfy us at the time but ultimately would not be in our best interest, or that are wrong for some other reason.

Think about it. Does any good parent give a child everything that child wants? My parents certainly didn't! As a child, I wanted to eat all of my Halloween candy the night I got it, but they made me choose a few pieces and save the rest. As a teenager, I wanted to go to a party, and they wouldn't allow it. Of course, I thought it was cruel of them to deny my request at the time, but since there were drugs at the party and the police raided it, in hindsight I can see the wisdom of their decision.

In the same way, I can look back over my life and think of things I asked God for that I desperately wanted at the time, but now am glad I didn't get. Yes, there are other things I wanted that God didn't give me and I still don't understand why, but I know that God sees the bigger picture, and gives me what I need, which isn't always what I want.

I also know that God's door is opened to anyone who knocks. When we search for God, we find God, not only in heaven but all around us and within us. God is everywhere; we just need to open our eyes, minds, and hearts to see and appreciate the good things God gives us every day.

Questions for Personal Reflection

1. How do you knock on God's door? What do you ask for?

2. How do you react when God gives you what you want? How about when you don't get what you asked for?

3. What are the good things that God has given you?

"Peter answered him, 'Lord, if it is you, command me to come to you on the water.' He said, 'Come.' So Peter got out of the boat, started walking on the water, and came toward Jesus. But when he noticed the strong wind, he became frightened, and beginning to sink, he cried out, 'Lord, save me!' Jesus immediately reached out his hand and caught him, saying to him, 'You of little faith, why did you doubt?' When they got into the boat, the wind ceased. And those in the boat worshipped him, saying 'Truly you are the Son of God.'"

Matthew 14:28-33

This incident happened after Jesus sent the disciples ahead in the boat without him, so he could be alone to pray. When he is ready to join them, their boat is far from land, being battered by waves, so he walks on the water toward them. The disciples are frightened and at first think he is a ghost, so Peter wants proof that it really is Jesus.

While we aren't likely to see Jesus walking on water or have him command us to do so, we do get frightened and battered by the waves of life, and God often offers help in ways we least expect. We want to reach out in trust and gratitude to accept God's outstretched hand, but first we want proof that it is indeed God guiding us. Sometimes what God tells us to do seems so outrageous, impossible even, that we aren't willing to get out of our boat and head toward God. Even when our present reality leaves a lot to be desired, it can seem more comfortable and less frightening than obeying Christ's command to do something we've never done before and aren't at all sure we'll be able to accomplish.

At other times, like Peter, we start walking in the right direction - toward Christ - but lose our courage and start sinking. Just as Jesus immediately reached out his hand to catch Peter, he reaches out to save us in our times of fear and doubt. When we start to sink, Jesus catches us.

Fortunately, God acts to save us even when we don't recognize God's presence in our lives or fully believe that we can do what God calls us to do. Notice that the disciples worship Jesus and acknowledge him as the Son of God only *after* the wind ceases. Peter is frightened as he begins sinking, and Jesus immediately reaches out to save him, while asking, "You of little faith, why did you doubt?" We can rest assured that we don't have to pass any kind of faith test or prove our worthiness before God will save us; we are saved purely by the grace of God, and that is good news indeed!

Questions for Personal Reflection

1. Have you ever asked God to do something to prove that God was real? If so, how did God respond?

2. If you had been there, would you have stayed in the boat or tried to walk on water? How do you usually respond when God asks you to do something unexpected?

3. How has Jesus acted to save you in the midst of your fear and doubt?

"Above all, maintain constant love for one another, for love covers a multitude of sins. Be hospitable to one another without complaining. Like good stewards of the manifold grace of God, serve one another with whatever gift each of you has received. Whoever speaks must do so as one speaking the very words of God; whoever serves must do so with the strength that God supplies, so that God may be glorified in all things through Jesus Christ. To him belong the glory and the power forever and ever. Amen."

1Peter 4:8-11

Maintaining constant love for one another does indeed cover a multitude of sins; just ask anyone who's been married for a long time! I've been happily married for more than twenty years, and there have certainly been times along the way when my husband Steve and I have said or done hurtful things to each other. Our love has always made it possible to forgive each other and move forward together.

These words weren't written to a couple, though; they were written to a Christian community. It's a lot harder to maintain love and be hospitable to one another without complaining when you don't get to choose the people in your community, and within it there are very different ideas about what God wants and opposing views on political and social issues.

It can be done, though, if we follow the guidelines mentioned in the verses following the commands to love one another and be hospitable to all. First, we are told to be good stewards of God's grace, and use the gifts we have to serve one another. In other words, recognize that no one is perfect, we are all saved by grace, not our own actions, and seek to use the gifts God has given us to help each other.

The next key is to speak as one speaking the very words of God. Obviously, this does not mean to see ourselves as God, and assume that God shares any view we express! Instead, we are called to ask ourselves if what we are about to say is true to the teachings and example of the God we claim to follow, and remember that we are supposed to model Christ-like behavior.

In conjunction with that, whoever serves is to do so with the strength that God supplies. In fact, I think we need strength from God just to make it through the day, let alone to resist our desire to be served and serve others instead.

The reason for doing all of these things is clear: so that God may be glorified in all things through Jesus Christ. We are all God's creations, and our ultimate goal should always be to glorify God by treating everyone we encounter with the grace and love that God has shown to each of us.

Questions for Personal Reflection

1. How do you show love for others, act hospitably, and serve them?

2. What are the gifts that you have received from God?

3. How does God supply you with strength, and how is God glorified in your words and deeds?

"People were bringing even infants to him that he might touch them; and when the disciples saw it, they sternly ordered them not to do it. But Jesus called for them and said, 'Let the little children come to me, and do not stop them; for it is to such as these that the kingdom of God belongs. Truly I tell you, whoever does not receive the kingdom of God as a little child will never enter it.'"

Luke 18:15-17

I love to watch young children. Some of my favorite places to observe them are theme parks where they get to meet their favorite cartoon characters, zoos and aquariums where they are so excited to watch the animals and eagerly point out what they see to their parents and anyone else who will listen, and in worship where they do things like clap and yell, "Yay, Mom" when Mom has just sung a beautiful solo, or collect the communion cups from everyone and see how tall they can stack them.

What does it mean to receive the kingdom of God as a little child? I think it means to have the same absolute honesty and trusting nature that young children typically have. I will never forget one family vacation when one of my sisters, who was about three years old at the time, struck up a conversation with an older gentleman on the shuttle bus. She ended up sitting next to him, and didn't hesitate to ask him personal questions and tell him about her life. When we reached our destination, she asked him if she could go home with him!

Needless to say, my mom vetoed that option and later warned her about getting too close to strangers. Not every person we encounter has our best interests in mind, and as we grow up we learn that it is not always safe or wise to be completely open and share our deepest thoughts and feelings, especially with someone we have just met. God, however, is the one who created us, knows everything about us, and wants us to be fully honest and trust God to accept us just as we are and encourage us as we grow in faith. God will never mock our feelings, betray our confidence, or take advantage of us.

I also think receiving the kingdom of God as a little child means having the same unbridled enthusiasm, the same joyous excitement and sense of wonder that children show when experiencing something for the first time (or the thousandth time, if it is something they really love). You know how children can watch the same show, sing the same song, or ride the same ride over and over and never get tired of it? What if we could have that same level of joy and excitement every time we encounter God? Scripture tells us that the kingdom of God is around us and within; what if we celebrated that reality and were filled with awe every time we saw another example of God's presence in our lives? What if we had the same confident certainty that God can fix anything and make it all better that young children have about their parents?

The reality is that God is far better than even the best human parents could possibly be. God is never too tired to listen to us or too busy doing other things to pay attention to us. Our challenge, and our joy, is to see the signs of God's kingdom all around us with child-like wonder, and relate to God with the same level of trust and openness that young children display.

Questions for Personal Reflection

1. When was the last time you felt a sense of awe and wonder? Where were you, and who or what inspired those feelings?

2. Is it easier for you to see the kingdom of God around you or within you? How do you enter that kingdom?

3. Do you think of God as your parent? Is that image comforting or frightening to you?

"O Lord, you have searched me and known me. You know when I sit down and when I rise up; you discern my thoughts from far away. You search out my path and my lying down, and are acquainted with all my ways…If I take the wings of the morning and settle at the farthest limits of the sea, even there your hand shall lead me, and your right hand shall hold me fast. If I say, 'Surely the darkness shall cover me, and the light around me become night,' even the darkness is not dark to you; the night is as bright as the day, for darkness is as light to you. For it was you who formed my inward parts; you knit me together in my mother's womb. I praise you, for I am fearfully and wonderfully made. Wonderful are your works; that I know very well."

Psalm 139:1-3, 9-14

I am the oldest of six kids, and my sister who is closest in age to me was my arch rival in our younger days. We regularly exchanged vicious verbal insults and sometimes fought physically. My greatest weapon was my long fingernails, and I regularly got in trouble for scratching her. One day, though, she decided to scratch herself and then blame me, so after she had plenty of scratch marks and was bleeding, she ran crying to Mom and claimed I had attacked her. Mom was wise enough to see through that, though, so instead of getting me in trouble, my sister got herself in trouble and also had to endure the pain from her self-inflicted wounds.

I mention that because we were both amazed that Mom could see the truth of what had happened so quickly. She knew us both well enough to figure it out quite easily. As this Psalm reminds us, God knows each of us even better than that. God can tell what we are thinking, and is familiar with all of our ways. No matter where we go, God goes with us, even to "the farthest limits of the sea."

This Psalm also reminds us that we are wonderful works of God. Many of us have trouble seeing ourselves that way. I once preached a sermon on the importance of loving ourselves, and asking God for forgiveness when we treat ourselves badly, and many people thanked me for it, even weeks later. I shared my own struggle with low self-esteem, and the fact that I have a harsh inner critic who demands perfection and constantly reminds me of all of the ways in which I am not good enough, and that resonated with a lot of listeners. The reality is that God created us very good, loves us, and continues to go with us and watch over us even when we ignore God or try to push God away.

Questions for Personal Reflection

1. Are you comforted or frightened by the idea of God searching and knowing you, discerning your thoughts, and being acquainted with all of your ways?

2. Have you ever tried to run away from God? What were the circumstances, and what brought you back to God?

3. Do you see yourself as one of God's wonderful creations?

"They heard the sound of the Lord God walking in the garden at the time of the evening breeze, and the man and his wife hid themselves from the presence of the Lord God among the trees of the garden. But the Lord God called to the man, and said to him, 'Where are you?' He said, 'I heard the sound of you in the garden, and I was afraid, because I was naked; and I hid myself. He said, 'Who told you that you were naked? Have you eaten from the tree of which I commanded you not to eat? The man said, 'The woman whom you gave to be with me, she gave me fruit from the tree and I ate.' Then the Lord God said to the woman, 'What is this that you have done?' The woman said, 'The serpent tricked me, and I ate.'"

Genesis 3:8-13

Sometimes we try to hide from God, because we are ashamed or afraid. That tendency goes all the way back to Adam and Eve, who hid among the trees in the Garden of Eden after they had eaten the forbidden fruit, so God wouldn't see them naked. Today, we don't usually worry about God literally seeing us naked, but we are sometimes hesitant to be naked emotionally before God. We may afraid to express our anger at God, or afraid of God knowing what we are thinking, or afraid of God finding out what we have said or done. Even though part of us knows that God is already aware of all of our thoughts, feelings, and actions, we are still reluctant to have an honest conversation with God about them.

Notice that when Adam and Eve are confronted by God, they don't simply admit what they have done and ask for forgiveness. Instead, they each blame someone else for making them do it. Adam blames Eve, and even God, when he says, "The woman *you* gave to be with me, *she* gave me fruit from the tree and I ate." Eve says, "The serpent tricked me." Neither is willing to take responsibility for their actions.

How often do we do the same thing? We claim that someone else persuaded us to do something we knew was wrong, and we had to go along because we didn't want to get teased, or lose friends, or lose our job, or ruin the reputation of an institution. Even when we are clearly at fault, we sometimes blame others; a fast food chain gets sued because a woman spilled hot coffee on her lap while driving, or a homeowner gets sued because a burglar injured himself on their property while trying to escape.

God didn't buy Adam and Eve's excuses; each of them had to face consequences (see Genesis 3:14-20). However, God also showed mercy; Genesis 3:21 states that God made garments of skins for them and clothed them. The reality is that we can't hide from God, and while that truth may scare us at times, it is also reassuring. God knows everything about us, loves us anyway, and refuses to give up on us.

Questions for Personal Reflection

1. In what ways do you try to hide from God?

2. Do you tend to blame others for your mistakes or take full responsibility for your actions?

3. How has God shown mercy to you?

"Our soul waits for the Lord; he is our help and shield. Our heart is glad in him, because we trust in his holy name. Let your steadfast love, O Lord, be upon us, even as we hope in you."

Psalm 33:20-22

I chose this text for the final meditation because it sums up nicely the messages I have tried to convey throughout this book. There are several key points highlighted in the verses above that I believe are especially important to keep in mind during the trying times we face as individuals, citizens of troubled nations, and members of the human race.

First, we are reminded that the Lord is our help and shield. Even the best human leaders, those who genuinely care about the people they serve and make decisions based on the common good, have their limitations, and if we rely on them to save us we are sure to be disappointed. Our own efforts don't always yield the hoped for results, either. Currently in the United States there is one job opening for every four people seeking employment, so obviously some of those who are diligently searching for work will not get hired. Ultimately, we need a power greater than any human, a loving God who has a vision for a better world and can inspire all of us to see each other as brothers and sisters and work together both to provide immediate aid to the neediest among us and to change the laws and policies that have caused so much suffering for so many people and done so much damage to the planet we call home.

Next, we are reminded that our hearts are glad because we trust in God's holy name. It can be challenging to be glad when times are tough, but trusting in God makes it possible to feel a joy that transcends our troubles. There is a peace that only God can give, a peace that can fill us with happiness even as we grieve our losses and face an uncertain future.

Finally, we draw strength from God's steadfast love. In a world in which changes seem to happen instantaneously, with little or no advance warning, and in which we must continuously adapt to new technology, new circumstances, and new leaders, it is comforting and reassuring to have something constant and unchanging on which to rely. God's steadfast love does indeed endure forever, and that makes it possible for us to endure even the most troubled times imaginable. We know that we do not face those times alone, and our trust in God's promises allows us to hold on to hope and help others do the same. Thanks be to God!

Questions for Personal Reflection

1. In what ways has God helped or shielded you and your family?

2. What does it mean to you to trust in God's holy name? Which name for God (Father, Lord God Almighty, Emmanuel, Messiah, Christ, Prince of Peace, Advocate, Holy Comforter, etc.) is most meaningful to you?

Sources and Notes

The quotes from John Klimakos (on page 65), Mark the Ascetic (page 67), and John of Dalyutha (page 69) are all taken from the following work:

McCuckin, J. A. (2002). *The Book of Mystical Chapters: Meditations on the Soul's Ascent from the Desert Fathers and Other Early Christian Contemplatives.* Boston: Shambhala Publications, Inc.

1. Page 18, Number 7.

2. Page 22, Number 15.

3. Page 25, Number 19.

The quote from Meister Eckhart (page 79) is taken from:

Inge, W. R. (1904). *Light, Life, and Love: Selections from the German Mystics of the Middle Ages.*

4. "Rest Only in God," page 22

Alphabetical Index of Scriptures Used

14853097R00065

Made in the USA
Charleston, SC
04 October 2012